KENNETH COX

DANIEL

PURE AND SIMPLE

KENNETH COX

DANIEL
PURE AND SIMPLE

*Written for anyone who wants to
understand the book of Daniel*

3ABN
books

Kenneth Cox Ministries

Dedication

Dedicated to the **_wise_** who understand.

Table of Contents

Icons to Watch For

There are three icons to identify the explanations:

 Certain texts offer a deeper insight into God's Word. In these cases, this icon is used: **"Consider This."**

 As history or events open up the understanding of a particular Scripture, this icon is used: **"Closer Look."**

 There are principles for understanding Bible prophecy that are consistent throughout Scripture. In these cases, this icon is used: **"Key to Prophecy."**

Why Study the Book of Daniel?

Prophecy and miracles distinguish the Bible from any other book. If we remove these two important features from the Scriptures, it takes away the hand of God in the affairs of man, and leaves him wondering, "Does God really care?" The book of Daniel is so sweeping, yet specific, in its prophecies, that a person must either accept it as being inspired, or reject it for being fraudulent.

Many critics have said that Daniel himself could not have written the book of Daniel, because he mentions too many things that happened after his death. They try to place the writing of Daniel in the second century B.C., rather than in the sixth century B.C. Even if Daniel had lived during the second century B.C., his prophesies would still concern the last day events. In fact, his prophesies come all the way down to the present time, and onward to the Second Coming of Jesus Christ. In addition, the detailed descriptions Daniel gave of the things that were happening in the sixth century B.C., show that he did live during that period of time.

One of the most important points in establishing the credibility of Daniel's prophecies is that Jesus Christ Himself accepted Daniel as being inspired, and quoted him in Matthew 24:15, " 'Therefore when you see the abomination of desolation, spoken of by Daniel the prophet, standing in the holy place' (whoever reads, let him understand)." To the Christian believer, Jesus' testimony should stand as convincing evidence.

Once one accepts the book of Daniel as being inspired, all Scripture falls into place. All the prophecies of Daniel are repeated in the book of Revelation, and they help us to see clearly what is taking place today. The book of Daniel is a book of prophecy; whereas the book of Revelation is just what its title states it is, a "revelation." As you read through the chapters of Daniel, you will see the hand of God pointing out the destiny of nations, and that will give you a solid foundation upon which to build your faith. Speaking of the Holy Scriptures, 2 Timothy 3:15 states that they are "... able to make you wise for salvation through faith which is in Christ Jesus."

Acknowledgments

I am convinced that the Word of God is its own interpreter, and that through study, the Holy Spirit will bring to our minds the meaning of the texts in Scripture. I am grateful for God's mercy and kindness to me, for it is through the conviction of the Holy Spirit that I have written this book on Daniel. There is nothing new under the sun, so I am indebted to the thoughts and ideas shared by the hundreds of men and women who have been led by the Spirit in their writing of books and papers on Daniel, and to the great number of sermons I have listened to. To those who have stood by my side, encouraging me, supporting me and lifting me up, I am eternally beholden. I was told that the more people who edit your book, the better off you are; so to the following I say a great big THANK YOU.

Diane Loer, Lindi McDougal, Carol Nielsen, Dona Klein, Bobby Davis, Bob Hablutzel, Pastor Steve Gifford, Dr. Samuel Nunez, Dr. Hugo Leon. A special thank you to Chrystique Neibauer for the graphics and layout.

Introduction

Can anyone who writes a book concerning Scripture understand it all at once? No!

If we read the Word of God a thousand times, will we see things we have never seen before? Yes! God's light will continue to shine brighter each time we study, and so it will be throughout eternity. Since God is Infinite and Omniscient, we will ever-continue to learn. The study of Daniel is a growth experience. As we study the prophecies given to Daniel, the Lord will continue to open our understanding. We must walk by faith in what we learn, and have learned. With the passage of time, some of Daniel's teachings have become clearer and more sure than ever before, and this has given them new meaning, leading to renewed hope.

Without question, Daniel 11 is the most difficult chapter of the Bible to understand. Although I have tried to make it readable and easy to grasp, God has promised, in answer to our prayers, to send us the Holy Spirit to enlighten our minds: *"However, when He, the Spirit of truth, has come, He will guide you into all truth …"* (John 16:13). Chapter twelve is the most controversial chapter in Daniel, yet it is probably the most important chapter because it concerns those of us who are living in the last days. There are two dangers we must strive to avoid: we must not interpret verses that apply to the end time (our day) as though they relate only to the past, and we must not apply verses to our day that do not apply to the end time. Again, much prayer should accompany the study of Daniel; pray that we will have the faith and courage to follow what we learn, and that it will help us to prepare our hearts for the coming of the Lord.

I have tried to keep this book brief, clear, and easy to understand. All the Scripture references pertain to the book of Daniel, unless otherwise stated. The Bible translation used is the New King James version.

How to Use This Book

How Do We Begin?

1. First, read each chapter in its entirety.

2. Then go back and re-read the texts, with their explanations.

Note: An icon is placed where an explanation is given, along with the texts that are being explained. If you follow the explanations in order, it will help to clarify many of the points in question.

It is my hope that this book will help you see the unerring accuracy of God's Word, and His wonderful love and care for mankind. Above all, it is my prayer that you will be led to accept Jesus Christ as your personal Savior.

PERSONALITY PROFILE
DANIEL

Also Known As: Belteshazzar—Babylonian name means, "Bel Provides".
Daniel—Hebrew name means, "God is Judge".

Home: Judea, but most of Daniel's life was spent in Babylon.

Family: Nothing is told about his family, except that he was of royal birth from the tribe of Judah.

Occupation: Statesman, Prophet and Prime Minister of two nations (Babylonian and Persian Empires).

Special Interests: The prophecies concerning the Jewish people and their return to Jerusalem, and which also refer to the followers of the Lord at the time of the end.

Best Known Today As: The author of the book of Daniel.

Daniel the Statesman

Of all the personalities in Scripture, only two are represented as being without fault: Joseph and Daniel. They stand alone as examples of lives that were totally committed to God. Ezekiel was a contemporary of Daniel's, and referred to him as being righteous in Ezekiel 14:14.

Daniel was between fifteen and eighteen years of age when he was taken captive to Babylon. There, he received an education in the culture and wisdom of the Chaldeans. Daniel was without rival in physical strength, appearance, mental vigor and literary attainment, as well as in spiritual power and insight. In fact, King Nebuchadnezzar found him to be ten times wiser in wisdom and understanding than all the magicians and astrologers in the realm.

Daniel is an example of what the power of God can accomplish in the life of an individual who is dedicated to following Him. In character, Daniel was true, noble, and generous, desiring to be at peace with all men. However, in matters of faith and lifestyle, he was firm and unchanging. Even in pagan courts, where practically everything he encountered was contrary to his beliefs, Daniel remained faithful to God.

Daniel held high positions in the courts of both Babylon and Medo-Persia, yet he faithfully served his God. He was neither proud, nor self-sufficient. Ever aware of his great need for God's wisdom and direction in his life, Daniel prayed three times a day, seeking the blessing of heaven to refresh his soul.

Daniel carried a great burden on his heart for his people Israel, the people of God. The visions he received while on the banks of the great rivers Shinar, Ulai, and Hiddekel were given especially for those of us living today. All around us we can see Daniel's prophecies being fulfilled, and "... *the wise shall understand*" (Daniel 12:10). Because of his integrity and devotion to God, Daniel was a man "greatly beloved" of Heaven.

DANIEL
PURE AND SIMPLE

CHAPTER 1

Introduction:
Daniel and Friends

DANIEL 1

1 In the third year of the reign of Jehoiakim king of Judah, Nebuchadnezzar king of Babylon came to Jerusalem and besieged it. 2 And the Lord gave Jehoiakim king of Judah into his hand, with some of the articles of the house of God, which he carried into the land of Shinar to the house of his god; and he brought the articles into the treasure house of his god. 3 Then the king instructed Ashpenaz, the master of his eunuchs, to bring some of the children of Israel and some of the king's descendants and some of the nobles, 4 young men in whom there was no blemish, but good-looking, gifted in all wisdom, possessing knowledge and quick to understand, who had ability to serve in the king's palace, and whom they might teach the language and literature of the Chaldeans. 5 And the king appointed for them a daily provision of the king's delicacies and of the wine which he drank, and three years of training for them, so that at the end of that time they might serve before the king. 6 Now from among those of the sons of Judah were Daniel, Hananiah, Mishael, and Azariah.

7 To them the chief of the eunuchs gave names: he gave Daniel the name Belteshazzar; to Hananiah, Shadrach; to Mishael, Meshach; and to Azariah, Abed-Nego. 8 But Daniel purposed in his heart that he would not defile himself with the portion of the king's delicacies, nor with the wine which he drank; therefore he requested of the chief of the eunuchs that he might not defile himself. 9 Now God had brought Daniel into the favor and goodwill of the chief of the eunuchs. 10 And the chief of the eunuchs said to Daniel, "I fear my lord the king, who has appointed your food and drink. For why should he see your faces looking worse than the young men who are your age? Then you would endanger my head before the king." 11 So Daniel said to the steward whom the chief of the eunuchs had set over Daniel, Hananiah, Mishael, and Azariah, 12 "Please test your servants for ten days, and let them give us vegetables to eat and water to drink. 13 Then let our appearance be examined before you, and the appearance of the young men who eat the portion of the king's

delicacies; and as you see fit, so deal with your servants."

14 So he consented with them in this matter, and tested them ten days.

15 And at the end of ten days their features appeared better and fatter in flesh than all the young men who ate the portion of the king's delicacies.

16 Thus the steward took away their portion of delicacies and the wine that they were to drink, and gave them vegetables.

17 As for these four young men, God gave them knowledge and skill in all literature and wisdom; and Daniel had understanding in all visions and dreams.

18 Now at the end of the days, when the king had said that they should be brought in, the chief of the eunuchs brought them in before Nebuchadnezzar.

19 Then the king interviewed them, and among them all none was found like Daniel, Hananiah, Mishael, and Azariah; therefore they served before the king.

20 And in all matters of wisdom and understanding about which the king examined them, he found them ten times better than all the magicians and astrologers who were in all his realm.

21 Thus Daniel continued until the first year of King Cyrus.

CHAPTER 1

Daniel and His Friends Obey God

Daniel 1:1–2 — *Nebuchadnezzar's Capture of Jerusalem*

"In the third year of the reign of Jehoiakim king of Judah, Nebuchadnezzar king of Babylon came to Jerusalem and besieged it. And the Lord gave Jehoiakim king of Judah into his hand, with some of the articles of the house of God, which he carried into the land of Shinar to the house of his god; and he brought the articles into the treasure house of his god."

Consider This **The Beginning of the Babylonian Empire**

The Assyrian Empire lasted for over 300 years. Ashurbanipal, the last of its real monarchs, grew old, and his sons were not interested in assuming rule of the empire. With his death in 627 B.C., the Assyrian Empire became very unstable.

Nabopolassar, a governor over the Babylonian region, seized this opportunity to conquer Assyria, and to establish Babylonian rule. Forming an army in 612 B.C., he expanded his territory until he had overthrown the Assyrian Empire's capitol city of Nineveh, killing Sinsharishkun, the last of the Assyrian kings. A remnant of the Assyrians revolted, and took a stand at Carchemish.

Being in ill health, Nabopolassar called upon his son, Nebuchadnezzar, to lead his army and put down the Assyrian revolt in Carchemish. In the south, the Assyrian's ally, Pharaoh Necho of Egypt, went to the defense of Carchemish, believing that if he succeeded in defeating Nebuchadnezzar, he would be able to control the whole of Mesopotamia.

Meanwhile, good King Josiah of Judah went out to engage Pharaoh Necho in battle, but without first consulting the Lord. Had Josiah done so, God would have told him that Nebuchadnezzar was an instrument in His hands (2 Chronicles 35:20–24). Pharaoh Necho killed Josiah in the valley of Megiddo, only to be defeated by Nebuchadnezzar at Carchemish. Although Nebuchadnezzar hotly pursued the Egyptian Pharaoh, he decided to take Judah captive along the way.

Nebuchadnezzar received word that his father had died, and immediately returned to Babylon to ascend to the throne. Before leaving Jerusalem, he gave careful instructions to his lieutenants concerning the articles from the temple there, and what hostages they were to bring from Judah to Babylon.

aniel 1:3–7 — The Deportation of Youth to Babylon

"Then the king instructed Ashpenaz, the master of his eunuchs, to bring some of the children of Israel and some of the king's descendants and some of the nobles, young men in whom there was no blemish, but good-looking, gifted in all wisdom, possessing knowledge and quick to understand, who had ability to serve in the king's palace, and whom they might teach the language and literature of the Chaldeans. And the king appointed for them a daily provision of the king's delicacies and of the wine which he drank, and three years of training for them, so that at the end of that time they might serve before the king. Now from among those of the sons of Judah were Daniel, Hananiah, Mishael, and Azariah. To them the chief of the eunuchs gave names: he gave Daniel the name Belteshazzar; to Hananiah, Shadrach; to Mishael, Meshach; and to Azariah, Abed-Nego."

A Different Kind of Young Men

In choosing the type of young men he sought, Nebuchadnezzar asked for the three things the world considers most important: good looks, intelligence, and great social graces. However, the Bible tells us that the attributes God considers most worthy are honesty, integrity, and loyalty—and Daniel and his friends possessed them all.

University of Babylon

These young men were to have three years of training at the University of Babylon, where they would become proficient in languages and international law, and master the details of Babylonian religion and culture. This would not only make them excellent diplomats for the Babylonian Empire, but also rid them of their ties to their Hebrew God, and their loyalty to Judah. The king believed that these indoctrination techniques would accomplish that goal.

Chaldean Education (Daniel 1:4)

Learning the language and literature of the Chaldeans would help them forget the heritage and beliefs they had been taught as children. These young men were still impressionable, so now was the time to change their thinking. Nebuchadnezzar hoped that a daily diet of educated paganism would erase their past, and turn them into Babylonians.

A Sense of Obligation (Daniel 1:5)

What unique privilege it must have been to eat food from the king's table, and to drink his wine. Daniel and his friends never had it this good at home, and it wouldn't have been difficult to get used to such a life. Considering all the king was doing for them, it would have been easy for them to begin thinking that Nebuchadnezzar wasn't really such a bad fellow, after all!

Change Their Heritage (Daniel 1:7)

Their Hebrew names were a constant reminder that they had been dedicated to God by their parents. However, their new Babylonian names would help them forget about the God of their fathers, and turn them to the worship of the gods after whom they were now named.

Daniel meant, "God is my Judge," but Belteshazzar meant, "Bel protects his life."

Hananiah meant, "The Lord is gracious," but Shadrach meant, "Exalt Aku."

Mishael meant, "Who belongs to God," but Meshach meant, "Who is what Aku is."

Azariah meant, "The Lord is my Helper," but Abed-Nego meant, "The servant of Nebo."

Daniel 1:8–16 — *The Faithfulness of Daniel*

"But Daniel purposed in his heart that he would not defile himself with the portion of the king's delicacies, nor with the wine which he drank; therefore he requested of the chief of the eunuchs that he might not defile himself. Now God had brought Daniel into the favor and goodwill of the chief of the eunuchs. And the chief of the eunuchs said to Daniel, 'I fear my lord the king, who has appointed your food and drink. For why should he see your faces looking worse than the young men who are your age? Then you would endanger my head before the king.' So Daniel said to the steward whom the chief of the eunuchs had set over Daniel, Hananiah, Mishael, and Azariah, 'Please test your servants for ten days, and let them give us vegetables to eat and water to drink. Then let our appearance be examined before you, and the appearance of the young men who eat the portion of the king's delicacies; and as you see fit, so deal with your servants.' So he consented with them in this matter, and tested them ten days. And at the end of ten

days their features appeared better and fatter in flesh than all the young men who ate the portion of the king's delicacies. Thus the steward took away their portion of delicacies and the wine that they were to drink, and gave them vegetables."

An Uncompromising Life

Daniel was willing to have his name changed, and to receive a Babylonian education, but in two essential areas he refused to compromise. Daniel knew that to give in on these points would destroy his faith in God. His faith was built on Scripture, which he accepted as the inspired Word of God; and this gave Daniel a firm foundation for his faith in God.

Once a person establishes his belief in God, his witness must be consistent with his belief—and this determines one's lifestyle. Daniel knew he could not sacrifice his lifestyle and keep his belief; therefore, he chose not to eat the food or to drink the wine from the king's table.

Among the archeological discoveries from the city of Babylon are three clay tablets containing recipes from the Babylonian kitchens. Their menus were rich in fatty foods, marbled meat, eggs, lentils, honey, and mulled wine. Daniel and his companions chose diets that were low in fat, carbohydrates, sugar, and calories—a diet guaranteed to make them physically fit, and mentally sharp.

Give Up Their Belief (Daniel 1:8)

All the young Hebrew men had been taught not to eat unclean meats (Leviticus 11). They had also been forbidden to eat food that had been offered to a pagan god (Deuteronomy 7). In addition, those who used fermented wine were considered unwise (Proverbs 20:1). As a result, eating and drinking at the king's table would require relinquishing their belief in the Word of God. In order for the indoctrination process to succeed, this step was absolutely necessary.

Change of Lifestyle (Daniel 1:10)

A person's entire lifestyle must be changed for such an indoctrination technique to succeed, and we are told twice in Scripture of efforts made to change Daniel's lifestyle. In chapter 1, Daniel was told to change his eating habits, and in chapter 6, he was told to stop praying to his God each day. These methods were so effective that, out of approximately 50 to 70 young Hebrew men who were especially chosen to serve in the court of Babylon, only four survived the ordeal and kept their faith. How many young people who are sent to worldly universities today lose their faith and belief in God?

Daniel 1:17–21 — God Honors Daniel and Companions

"As for these four young men, God gave them knowledge and skill in all literature and wisdom; and Daniel had understanding in all visions and dreams. Now at the end of the days, when the king had said that they should be brought in, the chief of the eunuchs brought them in before Nebuchadnezzar. Then the king interviewed them, and among them all none was found like Daniel, Hananiah, Mishael, and Azariah; therefore they served before the king. And in all matters of wisdom and understanding about which the king examined them, he found them ten times better than all the magicians and astrologers who were in all his realm. Thus Daniel continued until the first year of King Cyrus."

Faith Rewarded

Daniel, Hananiah, Mishael, and Azariah graduated from the University of Babylon summa cum laude. Not only were they smart, but God had also given them gifts of the Holy Spirit, such as wisdom and knowledge. *"God … is a rewarder of those who diligently seek Him."* Hebrews 11:6.

Daniel's first test of these gifts comes in the second chapter.

DANIEL
PURE AND SIMPLE

CHAPTERS
2–7

Historical and Prophetic:
Original Language Aramaic

In chapters 2 and 7, the prophecy begins with Babylon and ends with the Kingdom of God, and is written in the Babylonian language of Aramaic.

DANIEL 2

1 Now in the second year of Nebuchadnezzar's reign, Nebuchadnezzar had dreams; and his spirit was so troubled that his sleep left him.

2 Then the king gave the command to call the magicians, the astrologers, the sorcerers, and the Chaldeans to tell the king his dreams. So they came and stood before the king.

3 And the king said to them, "I have had a dream, and my spirit is anxious to know the dream."

4 Then the Chaldeans spoke to the king in Aramaic, "O king, live forever! Tell your servants the dream, and we will give the interpretation."

5 The king answered and said to the Chaldeans, "My decision is firm: if you do not make known the dream to me, and its interpretation, you shall be cut in pieces, and your houses shall be made an ash heap.

6 However, if you tell the dream and its interpretation, you shall receive from me gifts, rewards, and great honor. Therefore tell me the dream and its interpretation."

7 They answered again and said, "Let the king tell his servants the dream, and we will give its interpretation."

8 The king answered and said, "I know for certain that you would gain time, because you see that my decision is firm:

9 if you do not make known the dream to me, there is only one decree for you! For you have agreed to speak lying and corrupt words before me till the time has changed. Therefore tell me the dream, and I shall know that you can give me its interpretation."

10 The Chaldeans answered the king, and said, "There is not a man on earth who can tell the king's matter; therefore no king, lord, or ruler has ever asked such things of any magician, astrologer, or Chaldean.

11 It is a difficult thing that the king requests, and there is no other who can tell it to the king except the gods, whose dwelling is not with flesh."

12 For this reason the king was angry and very furious, and gave the command to destroy all the wise men of Babylon.

13 So the decree went out, and they began killing the wise men; and they sought Daniel and his companions, to kill them.

14 Then with counsel and wisdom Daniel answered Arioch, the captain of the king's guard, who had gone out to kill the wise men of Babylon;

15 he answered and said to Arioch the king's captain, "Why is the decree from the king so urgent?" Then Arioch made the decision known to Daniel.

16 So Daniel went in and asked the king to give him time, that he might tell the king the interpretation.

17 Then Daniel went to his house, and made the decision known to Hananiah, Mishael, and Azariah, his companions,

18 that they might seek mercies from the God of heaven concerning this secret, so that Daniel and his companions might not perish with the rest of the wise men of Babylon.

19 Then the secret was revealed to Daniel in a night vision. So Daniel blessed the God of heaven.

20 Daniel answered and said:

"Blessed be the name of God forever and ever,

For wisdom and might are His.

21 And He changes the times and the seasons;

He removes kings and raises up kings;

He gives wisdom to the wise

And knowledge to those who have understanding.

22 He reveals deep and secret things;

He knows what is in the darkness,

And light dwells with Him.

23 "I thank You and praise You,

O God of my fathers;

You have given me wisdom and might,

And have now made known to me what we asked of You,

For You have made known to us the king's demand."

24 Therefore Daniel went to Arioch, whom the king had appointed to destroy the wise men of Babylon. He went and said thus to him: "Do not destroy the wise men of Babylon; take me before the king, and I will tell the king the interpretation."

25 Then Arioch quickly brought Daniel before the king, and said thus to him, "I have found a man of the captives of Judah, who will make known to the king the interpretation."

26 The king answered and said to Daniel, whose name was Belteshazzar, "Are you able to make known to me the dream which I have seen, and its interpretation?"

27 Daniel answered in the presence of the king, and said, "The secret which the king has demanded, the wise men, the astrologers, the magicians, and the soothsayers cannot declare to the king.

28 But there is a God in heaven who reveals secrets, and He has made known to King Nebuchadnezzar what will be in the latter days. Your dream, and the visions of your head upon your bed, were these:

29 As for you, O king, thoughts came to your mind while on your bed, about what would come to pass after this; and He who reveals secrets has made known to you what will be.

30 But as for me, this secret has not been revealed to me because I have more wisdom than anyone living, but for our sakes who make known the interpretation to the king, and that you may know the thoughts of your heart.

31 "You, O king, were watching; and behold, a great image! This great image, whose splendor was excellent, stood before you; and its form was awesome.

32 This image's head was of fine gold, its chest and arms of silver, its belly and thighs of bronze,

33 its legs of iron, its feet partly of iron and partly of clay.

34 You watched while a stone was cut out without hands, which struck the image on its feet of iron and clay, and broke them in pieces.

35 Then the iron, the clay, the bronze, the silver, and the gold were crushed together, and became like chaff from the summer threshing floors; the wind carried them away so that no trace of them was found. And the stone that struck the image became a great mountain and filled the whole earth.

36 "This is the dream. Now we will tell the interpretation of it before the king.

37 You, O king, are a king of kings. For the God of heaven has given you a kingdom, power, strength, and glory;

38 and wherever the children of men dwell, or the beasts of the field and the birds of the heaven, He has given them into your hand, and has made you ruler over them all—you are this head of gold.

39 But after you shall arise another kingdom inferior to yours; then another, a third kingdom of bronze, which shall rule over all the earth.

40 And the fourth kingdom shall be as strong as iron, inasmuch as iron breaks in pieces and shatters everything; and like iron that crushes, that kingdom will break in pieces and crush all the others.

41 Whereas you saw the feet and toes, partly of potter's clay and partly of iron, the kingdom shall be divided; yet the strength of the iron shall be in it, just as you saw the iron mixed with ceramic clay.

42 And as the toes of the feet were partly of iron and partly of clay, so the kingdom shall be partly strong and partly fragile.

43 As you saw iron mixed with ceramic clay, they will mingle with the seed of men; but they will not adhere to one another, just as iron does not mix with clay.

44 And in the days of these kings the God of heaven will set up a kingdom which shall never be destroyed; and the kingdom shall not be left to other people; it shall break in pieces and consume all these kingdoms, and it shall stand forever.

45 Inasmuch as you saw that the stone was cut out of the mountain without hands, and that it broke in pieces the iron, the bronze, the clay, the silver, and the gold—the great God has made known to the king what will come to pass after this. The dream is certain, and its interpretation is sure."

46 Then King Nebuchadnezzar fell on his face, prostrate before Daniel, and commanded that they should present an offering and incense to him.

47 The king answered Daniel, and said, "Truly your God is the God of gods, the Lord of kings, and a revealer of secrets, since you could reveal this secret."

48 Then the king promoted Daniel and gave him many great gifts; and he made him ruler over the whole province of Babylon, and chief administrator over all the wise men of Babylon.

49 Also Daniel petitioned the king, and he set Shadrach, Meshach, and Abed-Nego over the affairs of the province of Babylon; but Daniel sat in the gate of the king.

CHAPTER 2

Nebuchadnezzar's Dream

Inside this Chapter

This section of the book of Daniel begins and ends with the same Prophecy, written in the Aramaic language.

The prophecy in Daniel 2 is foundational to understanding the rest of the prophecies in this book. This prophecy was given to Nebuchadnezzar, not to Daniel. It is a test of the gift God gave Daniel, granting him *"...understanding in all visions and dreams."* Daniel 1:17.

Because of his ability and his faithfulness to God, Daniel was promoted to the very top of the Babylonian kingdom; to a position in which he could both witness to the pagan Babylonians, and help the Jewish nation in captivity. Since the seventh chapter repeats this prophecy, and enlarges upon it, understanding Daniel 2 makes Daniel 7 much more clear.

Daniel 2:1–3 — Nebuchadnezzar's Dream

"Now in the second year of Nebuchadnezzar's reign, Nebuchadnezzar had dreams; and his spirit was so troubled that his sleep left him. Then the king gave the command to call the magicians, the astrologers, the sorcerers, and the Chaldeans to tell the king his dreams. So they came and stood before the king. And the king said to them, 'I have had a dream, and my spirit is anxious to know the dream.'"

Nebuchadnezzar

God gave pagan, idolatrous King Nebuchadnezzar a dream, and then caused him to forget its details. Upon waking, all the king could remember was that the dream was very significant.

Nebuchadnezzar was proud, ruthless, and vindictive in dealing with his subjects. Yet he had an innate sense of justice, and of what was right. He was named after the pagan god Nabu, the Babylonian god of prophecy—yet neither his pagan god, nor his so-called "wise men," could tell him his dream, and then interpret it for him. Only the God in Heaven could make known to Nebuchadnezzar what the latter days would bring. Isaiah 44:24–25.

Nebuchadnezzar ruled Babylon for 40 years, and during that time God patiently revealed Himself to him, changing his heart.

The Chaldeans considered dreams to be omens of future events, and they expended great effort in understanding and interpreting them.

Babylon's magicians, astrologers, and sorcerers were supposed to be experts in that field. Archeological discoveries in Babylon have revealed libraries of clay tablets dedicated to explaining dreams; therefore, Nebuchadnezzar likely felt certain that his wise men would know the dream's interpretation.

Daniel 2:4–11 — Wise Men's Predicament

"Then the Chaldeans spoke to the king in Aramaic, 'O king, live forever! Tell your servants the dream, and we will give the interpretation.'

"The king answered and said to the Chaldeans, 'My decision is firm: if you do not make known the dream to me, and its interpretation, you shall be cut in pieces, and your houses shall be made an ash heap. However, if you tell the dream and its interpretation, you shall receive from me gifts, rewards, and great honor. Therefore tell me the dream and its interpretation.'

"They answered again and said, 'Let the king tell his servants the dream, and we will give its interpretation.'

"The king answered and said, 'I know for certain that you would gain time, because you see that my decision is firm: if you do not make known the dream to me, there is only one decree for you! For you have agreed to speak lying and corrupt words before me till the time has changed. Therefore tell me the dream, and I shall know that you can give me its interpretation.'

"The Chaldeans answered the king, and said, 'There is not a man on earth who can tell the king's matter; therefore no king, lord, or ruler has ever asked such things of any magician, astrologer, or Chaldean. It is a difficult thing that the king requests, and there is no other who can tell it to the king except the gods, whose dwelling is not with flesh.'"

Unreasonable Request

> **Consider This**

Anyone can invent an interpretation of a known dream, but telling a person their unknown dream is an entirely different matter. No one had ever made such a request. Nevertheless, his very demand was what saved the king from receiving a false interpretation. The fact that the king was firm in his decision did not allow the wise men any room for error, yet they could not decipher the dream unless they knew what the king had dreamed. Similarly, today we find people with worldly educations trying to interpret a prophecy in Scripture, or to explain a passage in the Bible—situations comparable to those "wise" men of Babylon trying to interpret the king's dream! *"But the natural man does not receive the things of the Spirit of God, for they are foolishness to him; nor can he know them, because they are spiritually discerned."* 1 Corinthians 2:14.

Daniel 2:12–15 — The King's Death Decree

"For this reason the king was angry and very furious, and gave the command to destroy all the wise men of Babylon. So the decree went out, and they began killing the wise men; and they sought Daniel and his companions, to kill them.

"Then with counsel and wisdom Daniel answered Arioch, the captain of the king's guard, who had gone out to kill the wise men of Babylon; he answered and said to Arioch the king's captain, 'Why is the decree from the king so urgent?' Then Arioch made the decision known to Daniel."

Too Young to Help, but Old Enough to Pay the Price

Consider This

Since Daniel and his friends were young men in their late teens, Nebuchadnezzar's command to call the wise men did not include them. He was looking for men of experience, not novices. Nevertheless, when the decree was given to destroy all the wise men of Babylon, they were included in it!

Daniel 2:16–23 — God Reveals the Dream

"So Daniel went in and asked the king to give him time, that he might tell the king the interpretation. Then Daniel went to his house, and made the decision known to Hananiah, Mishael, and Azariah, his companions, that they might seek mercies from the God of heaven concerning this secret, so that Daniel and his companions might not perish with the rest of the wise men of Babylon. Then the secret was revealed to Daniel in a night vision. So Daniel blessed the God of heaven.

"Daniel answered and said:

"'Blessed be the name of God forever and ever,

For wisdom and might are His.

And He changes the times and the seasons;

He removes kings and raises up kings;

He gives wisdom to the wise
And knowledge to those who have understanding.
He reveals deep and secret things;
He knows what is in the darkness,
And light dwells with Him.
I thank You and praise You,
O God of my fathers;
You have given me wisdom and might,
And have now made known to me what we asked of You,
For You have made known to us the king's demand.'"

Closer Look

Walking by Faith

Daniel risked his life in going before the king, yet if no one proved able to interpret the king's dream, he would lose his life anyway. Nebuchadnezzar had no choice but to see Daniel, since no one could explain his dream. Nebuchadnezzar was also no-doubt impressed with Daniel's character, so he granted him an audience. Daniel and his companions knew that only the God in Heaven could provide the information they required, so falling on their knees, they presented their need to Him. Then, trusting in the providence of Almighty God, they waited, and the answer came! With thanksgiving and praise in their hearts, they thanked God for His goodness and mercy to them.

Daniel 2:24–30 — Daniel Goes Before the King

"Therefore Daniel went to Arioch, whom the king had appointed to destroy the wise men of Babylon. He went and said thus to him: 'Do not destroy the wise men of Babylon; take me before the king, and I will tell the king the interpretation.'

"Then Arioch quickly brought Daniel before the king, and said thus to him, 'I have found a man of the captives of Judah, who will make known to the king the interpretation.'

"The king answered and said to Daniel, whose name was Belteshazzar, 'Are you able to make known to me the dream which I have seen, and its interpretation?'

"Daniel answered in the presence of the king, and said, 'The secret which

the king has demanded, the wise men, the astrologers, the magicians, and the soothsayers cannot declare to the king. But there is a God in heaven who reveals secrets, and He has made known to King Nebuchadnezzar what will be in the latter days. Your dream, and the visions of your head upon your bed, were these: As for you, O king, thoughts came to your mind while on your bed, about what would come to pass after this; and He who reveals secrets has made known to you what will be. But as for me, this secret has not been revealed to me because I have more wisdom than anyone living, but for our sakes who make known the interpretation to the king, and that you may know the thoughts of your heart.'"

The God in Heaven

Only by the intercession of Daniel were the wise men of Babylon saved from a cruel, disgraceful death. In his very first words Daniel disclaimed honor for himself; instead, he exalted the God of Heaven who had made known the dream. Nebuchadnezzar made the same request of Daniel that he had of the wise men, *"Are you able to make known to me the dream which I have seen, and its interpretation?"* To which Daniel replied, *"There is a God in heaven who reveals secrets, and He has made known to King Nebuchadnezzar what will be in the latter days."*

Daniel 2:31–35 — The Great Image

"You, O king, were watching; and behold, a great image! This great image, whose splendor was excellent, stood before you; and its form was awesome. This image's head was of fine gold, its chest and arms of silver, its belly and thighs of bronze, its legs of iron, its feet partly of iron and partly of clay. You watched while a stone was cut out without hands, which struck the image on its feet of iron and clay, and broke them in pieces. Then the iron, the clay, the bronze, the silver, and the gold were crushed together, and became like chaff from the summer threshing floors; the wind carried them away so that no trace of them was found. And the stone that struck the image became a great mountain and filled the whole earth."

The Rock of Ages

The image that Nebuchadnezzar saw was made of metals that decreased in value from gold to a mixture of iron and clay. However, the central theme of the book of Daniel is the Rock! The key figure in Nebuchadnezzar's dream was the Rock that destroyed the image, and grew into an earth-filling mountain—a kingdom that would never end.

Only the Hand of the Divine can outline in 15 short verses the history of the human race with absolute accuracy. The Scriptures have withstood the test of time, and it carries with it great meaning for us who live today.

Daniel 2:36–38 — Head of Gold

"This is the dream. Now we will tell the interpretation of it before the king. You, O king, are a king of kings. For the God of heaven has given you a kingdom, power, strength, and glory; and wherever the children of men dwell, or the beasts of the field and the birds of the heaven, He has given them into your hand, and has made you ruler over them all—you are this head of gold."

Babylon, 605 B.C.
The kingdom of Babylon lasted for 70 years. Nebuchadnezzar ruled for 40 of those years, which is why Scripture states, *"... you are this head of gold."* Daniel 2:38.

It is significant to note that history refers to Babylon as the "golden kingdom." Through the blessing of God, Babylon became the greatest kingdom on earth. Nebuchadnezzar lavished the wealth of many nations upon the city. The Seven Hanging Gardens, the Ishtar Gate, and the walls around the city were just some of its many spectacles to behold.

Daniel 2:39 — Arms and Chest of Silver

"But after you shall arise another kingdom inferior to yours..."

Medo-Persia, 539 B.C.
Just as silver is inferior to gold, the next kingdom was to be inferior to Babylon. In 539 B.C., Medo-Persia overthrew Babylon under the leadership of Cyrus the Great. It is very significant to note that God mentioned Cyrus by name one hundred years before he was born! God also described how Cyrus would overthrow the city of Babylon (Isaiah 45:1). This dramatic event is described in Daniel 5.

Since the Medo-Persian Empire was a coalition of two powers, Media and Persia, Scripture describes them as two arms of silver.

Daniel 2:39 — Belly and Thighs of Bronze

"...then another, a third kingdom of bronze, which shall rule over all the earth."

Closer Look

Greece, 331 B.C.

The thirty-ninth verse mentions two world powers, Medo-Persia and Greece. It is remarkable that the Scripture states Greece would rule over all the earth, for when this prophecy was given, Greece was only a weak and disorganized assortment of city-states.

True to the prophecy, in 331 B.C., at the Battle of Arbela, Alexander the Great faced Persia's Darius III. Alexander had only 40,000 soldiers; the army of Darius numbered one million! Yet God's word never fails. Alexander won the battle by implementing a new type of warfare, and he extended Greece's domain to the borders of India.

In Daniel 8:1–8, 20 and 21, the Bible identifies Medo-Persia and Greece by name.

Daniel 2:40 — Legs of Iron

"And the fourth kingdom shall be as strong as iron, inasmuch as iron breaks in pieces and shatters everything; and like iron that crushes, that kingdom will break in pieces and crush all the others."

Closer Look

Pagan Rome, 168 B.C.

Rome ruled longer than any world power. It defeated Greece in 168 B.C., and it reigned until 476 A.D. The Scripture refers to this power as being "strong as iron," and it is significant to note that history refers to it as the "Iron Monarchy of Rome." Defeating every nation in her path by brute force, Rome eventually succeeded in conquering the entire Mediterranean World, and Western Europe.

The Roman Empire consisted of two parts, Eastern Rome and Western Rome, which is why the image of Nebuchadnezzar's dream has two legs of iron. Although she ruled with an iron hand, Rome spread civilization to the world by making the roadways and waterways safe for travel.

It was not by chance that Jesus Christ was born at this time, for the message of a Savior was then able to rapidly spread to all humanity. In fact, Christianity went to the then-known world in just a few short years.

Daniel 2:41–42 — Feet and Toes

"Whereas you saw the feet and toes, partly of potter's clay and partly of iron, the kingdom shall be divided; yet the strength of the iron shall be in it, just as you saw the iron mixed with ceramic clay. And as the toes of the feet were partly of iron and partly of clay, so the kingdom shall be partly strong and partly fragile."

A Kingdom Divided, 476 A.D.

Only the Omniscient One could make a prediction such as this: *"... the kingdom shall be divided."* Rome, which had ruled longer than any other empire, was about to be broken apart.

To man's reasoning, this seemed to defy logic. Nevertheless, true to the Word of God, one of the greatest phenomena in history took place as masses of people suddenly began to move. In 476 A.D., the Goths (Barbarians) invaded, and divided, the Roman Empire. These Germanic peoples became the nations of Western Europe today:

Anglo-Saxons	England
Franks	France
Burgundians	Switzerland
Visigoths	Spain
Alamanni	Germany
Suevi	Portugal
Lombards	Italy
Heruli	Destroyed (493 A.D.)
Vandals	Destroyed (534 A.D.)
Ostrogoths	Destroyed (538 A.D.)

Daniel 7 explains why these last three nations were destroyed.

Daniel 2:43 — *Iron Mixed with Ceramic Clay*

"As you saw iron mixed with ceramic clay, they will mingle with the seed of men; but they will not adhere to one another, just as iron does not mix with clay."

Will Not Adhere to One Another

At least six times in recorded history, man has tried to prove God wrong.

Charlemagne, who tried to establish his Holy Roman Empire, died a disappointed man.

Charles V hoped to unite all Europe. He launched the continent into a blood-bath, and ended his days in seclusion in a convent.

Louis XIV of France established his famous Sunrise Kingdom to engulf all Europe, but it fell apart.

Napoleon Bonaparte said, "Europe will soon become one nation," but he was defeated, and poisoned.

This brings us to the time of Kaiser Wilhelm of Germany. As the Scripture foretold, " ... *they will mingle with the seed of men,*" which is an old English term meaning "to intermarry."

At that time, nearly all the European heads of state had intermarried in an attempt to unify Europe. True to the prophecy, however, their nations did not *"adhere to one another."* This resulted in World War I which, as one historian put it, *"... was nothing but a big family argument."*

Still unconvinced, Adolf Hitler decided that he would not just rule Europe, but the entire world! Establishing his so-called Thousand Year Reich, he was joined by Japan and Italy, and the world found itself in World War II. Eventually, Hitler committed suicide, two atomic bombs were dropped on Japan, and Italy's Mussolini was hanged.

In light of such overwhelming evidence that God is the Bible's Author, how can any person reasonably refuse to believe it?

No Kingdom As Yet

Nebuchadnezzar's dream has stood the test of time; however, today it carries special significance because it concerns the latter days—the time in which we live.

A careful study of Daniel and Revelation reveals that the ten toes of

Daniel 2, are the same ten kings mentioned in Revelation 17:12, *"which have received no kingdom as yet."* Further study of Revelation 17 reveals that *"as yet"* refers to an exact time period. Also, please note the Bible states that the ten kings have received *"no kingdom (singular) as yet"*; it does not say they haven't yet received their *"kingdoms"* (plural).

The modern nations of Western Europe have been kingdoms since the breakup of the Roman Empire, however, they have not *"as yet"* spoken with *"one mind,"* as Revelation 17:13 states they will. They will receive power from, or have some type of alliance with, the *"beast,"* during a short period referred to as *"one hour."* This will happen just before the Second Coming of Jesus.

We will examine in detail the identity of this *"beast"* power in subsequent chapters. We will discover that during this *"one hour"* period, *"these nations of Europe will have *"one mind,"* and *"will give their power and authority to the beast."* Revelation 17:13. It is significant to note that the European Community is already taking steps in that direction.

Daniel 2:44–45 — In the Days of These Kings

"And in the days of these kings the God of heaven will set up a kingdom which shall never be destroyed; and the kingdom shall not be left to other people; it shall break in pieces and consume all these kingdoms, and it shall stand forever. Inasmuch as you saw that the stone was cut out of the mountain without hands, and that it broke in pieces the iron, the bronze, the clay, the silver, and the gold—the great God has made known to the king what will come to pass after this. The dream is certain, and its interpretation is sure."

Dream is Certain, Interpretation is Sure

Since 90 percent of the dream's interpretation has been absolutely accurate, we can be certain that the remaining 10 percent will be accurate as well! We are living in the days of *these kings*—the latter days—during the final events of this world's history, just before the Second Coming of Christ. The *"stone"* that fills *"the whole earth is the kingdom of God."* Matthew 12:28. Jesus will demolish all earthly powers in opposition to Him. Now, just before Jesus returns, each one of us must make sure that we are citizens of the Heavenly Kingdom!

Daniel 2:46–49 — Daniel's Promotion

"Then King Nebuchadnezzar fell on his face, prostrate before Daniel, and commanded that they should present an offering and incense to him. The king answered Daniel, and said, 'Truly your God is the God of gods, the Lord of kings, and a revealer of secrets, since you could reveal this secret.' Then the king promoted Daniel and gave him many great gifts; and he made him ruler over the whole province of Babylon, and chief administrator over all the wise men of Babylon. Also Daniel petitioned the king, and he set Shadrach, Meshach, and Abed-Nego over the affairs of the province of Babylon; but Daniel sat in the gate of the king."

Consider This — **The Revealer of Secrets**

Because of Daniel's interpretation of the dream, God placed him and his friends in high positions of leadership for the remainder of his reign. This gave the people of Babylon the opportunity to learn about the only true God, while it simultaneously gave the Jews the privilege of being a light unto the Gentiles.

Nebuchadnezzar would come face to face with *"the God of gods, the Lord of kings, and a revealer of secrets"* two more times.

DANIEL 3

1 Nebuchadnezzar the king made an image of gold, whose height was sixty cubits and its width six cubits. He set it up in the plain of Dura, in the province of Babylon.

2 And King Nebuchadnezzar sent word to gather together the satraps, the administrators, the governors, the counselors, the treasurers, the judges, the magistrates, and all the officials of the provinces, to come to the dedication of the image which King Nebuchadnezzar had set up.

3 So the satraps, the administrators, the governors, the counselors, the treasurers, the judges, the magistrates, and all the officials of the provinces gathered together for the dedication of the image that King Nebuchadnezzar had set up; and they stood before the image that Nebuchadnezzar had set up.

4 Then a herald cried aloud: "To you it is commanded, O peoples, nations, and languages,

5 that at the time you hear the sound of the horn, flute, harp, lyre, and psaltery, in symphony with all kinds of music, you shall fall down and worship the gold image that King Nebuchadnezzar has set up;

6 and whoever does not fall down and worship shall be cast immediately into the midst of a burning fiery furnace."

7 So at that time, when all the people heard the sound of the horn, flute, harp, and lyre, in symphony with all kinds of music, all the people, nations, and languages fell down and worshiped the gold image which King Nebuchadnezzar had set up.

8 Therefore at that time certain Chaldeans came forward and accused the Jews.

9 They spoke and said to King Nebuchadnezzar, "O king, live forever!

10 You, O king, have made a decree that everyone who hears the sound of the horn, flute, harp, lyre, and psaltery, in symphony with all kinds of music, shall fall down and worship the gold image;

11 and whoever does not fall down and worship shall be cast into the midst of a burning fiery furnace.

12 There are certain Jews whom you have set over the affairs of the province of Babylon: Shadrach, Meshach, and Abed-Nego; these men, O king, have not paid due regard to you. They do not serve your gods or worship the gold image which you have set up."

13 Then Nebuchadnezzar, in rage

and fury, gave the command to bring Shadrach, Meshach, and Abed-Nego. So they brought these men before the king.

14 Nebuchadnezzar spoke, saying to them, "Is it true, Shadrach, Meshach, and Abed-Nego, that you do not serve my gods or worship the gold image which I have set up?

15 Now if you are ready at the time you hear the sound of the horn, flute, harp, lyre, and psaltery, in symphony with all kinds of music, and you fall down and worship the image which I have made, good! But if you do not worship, you shall be cast immediately into the midst of a burning fiery furnace. And who is the god who will deliver you from my hands?"

16 Shadrach, Meshach, and Abed-Nego answered and said to the king, "O Nebuchadnezzar, we have no need to answer you in this matter.

17 If that is the case, our God whom we serve is able to deliver us from the burning fiery furnace, and He will deliver us from your hand, O king.

18 But if not, let it be known to you, O king, that we do not serve your gods, nor will we worship the gold image which you have set up."

19 Then Nebuchadnezzar was full of fury, and the expression on his face changed toward Shadrach, Meshach, and Abed-Nego. He spoke and commanded that they heat the furnace seven times more than it was usually heated.

20 And he commanded certain mighty men of valor who were in his army to bind Shadrach, Meshach, and Abed-Nego, and cast them into the burning fiery furnace.

21 Then these men were bound in their coats, their trousers, their turbans, and their other garments, and were cast into the midst of the burning fiery furnace.

22 Therefore, because the king's command was urgent, and the furnace exceedingly hot, the flame of the fire killed those men who took up Shadrach, Meshach, and Abed-Nego.

23 And these three men, Shadrach, Meshach, and Abed-Nego, fell down bound into the midst of the burning fiery furnace.

24 Then King Nebuchadnezzar was astonished; and he rose in haste and spoke, saying to his counselors, "Did we not cast three men bound into the midst of the fire?"

They answered and said to the king, "True, O king."

25 "Look!" he answered, "I see four men loose, walking in the midst of the fire; and they are not hurt, and the form of the fourth is like the Son of God."

26 Then Nebuchadnezzar went near the mouth of the burning fiery furnace and spoke, saying, "Shadrach, Meshach, and Abed-Nego, servants of the Most High God, come out, and come here." Then Shadrach, Meshach, and Abed-Nego came from the midst of the fire.

27 And the satraps, administrators, governors, and the king's counselors gathered together, and they saw these men on whose bodies the fire had no power; the hair of their head was not singed nor were their garments affected, and the smell of fire was not on them.

28 Nebuchadnezzar spoke, saying, "Blessed be the God of Shadrach, Meshach, and Abed-Nego, who sent His Angel and delivered His servants who trusted in Him, and they have frustrated the king's word, and yielded their bodies, that they should not serve nor worship any god except their own God!

29 Therefore I make a decree that any people, nation, or language which speaks anything amiss against the God of Shadrach, Meshach, and Abed-Nego shall be cut in pieces, and their houses shall be made an ash heap; because there is no other God who can deliver like this."

30 Then the king promoted Shadrach, Meshach, and Abed-Nego in the province of Babylon.

CHAPTER 3

Fiery Furnace

Inside this Chapter

Daniel 3:1–7 — *Nebuchadnezzar's Golden Image*

"Nebuchadnezzar the king made an image of gold, whose height was sixty cubits and its width six cubits. He set it up in the plain of Dura, in the province of Babylon. And King Nebuchadnezzar sent word to gather together the satraps, the administrators, the governors, the counselors, the treasurers, the judges, the magistrates, and all the officials of the provinces, to come to the dedication of the image which King Nebuchadnezzar had set up. So the satraps, the administrators, the governors, the counselors, the treasurers, the judges, the magistrates, and all the officials of the provinces gathered together for the dedication of the image that King Nebuchadnezzar had set up; and they stood before the image that Nebuchadnezzar had set up. Then a herald cried aloud: 'To you it is commanded, O peoples, nations, and languages, that at the time you hear the sound of the horn, flute, harp, lyre, and psaltery, in symphony with all kinds of music, you shall fall down and worship the gold image that King Nebuchadnezzar has set up; and whoever does not fall down and worship shall be cast immediately into the midst of a burning fiery furnace.'

"So at that time, when all the people heard the sound of the horn, flute, harp, and lyre, in symphony with all kinds of music, all the people, nations, and languages fell down and worshiped the gold image which King Nebuchadnezzar had set up."

How Quickly We Forget

This is the same king who just a short time before had said that Daniel's God was the "God of gods," and the "King of kings."

Because of Daniel, the lives of the wise men were spared. However, in an attempt to heal their wounded pride, these same wise men set out to convince Nebuchadnezzar that Daniel was wrong.

"This is Babylon the Great," they likely said. "Surely it isn't possible for an inferior kingdom to take its place."

In this way, they convinced Nebuchadnezzar that the entire image represented Babylon, and not just the head of gold. In an act of proud defiance against God, Nebuchadnezzar subsequently made an image of gold from head to toe, reflecting his desire that the entire image represented him, and his kingdom of Babylon.

The image was approximately 90 feet tall, and 9 feet wide. That disproportionate height-to-width ratio indicates that the height must have included the pedestal on which the image stood.

Images of great height were common in the ancient world. Egypt had many of them, but an image of solid gold would be most impressive, and it surely fed Nebuchadnezzar's pride and self-exaltation. What better way to impress upon the minds of the people his greatness, and that of his kingdom, than to have them all bow down together and worship the image?

Since music affects our emotions, it provided an ideal means to aid the king in accomplishing his objective.

Daniel 3:8–12 — Shadrach, Meshach, and Abed-Nego Stand Firm

"Therefore at that time certain Chaldeans came forward and accused the Jews. They spoke and said to King Nebuchadnezzar, 'O king, live forever! You, O king, have made a decree that everyone who hears the sound of the horn, flute, harp, lyre, and psaltery, in symphony with all kinds of music, shall fall down and worship the gold image; and whoever does not fall down and worship shall be cast into the midst of a burning fiery furnace. There are certain Jews whom you have set over the affairs of the province of Babylon: Shadrach, Meshach, and Abed-Nego; these men, O king, have not paid due regard to you. They do not serve your gods or worship the gold image which you have set up.'"

Consider This

Why Not Compromise?

These young Hebrew men had many potential reasons to compromise. After all, their very lives were on the line. How easily they could have reasoned, "What difference does it make? Everyone else is doing it. God knows what we really believe in our hearts. The king has been good to us, and we need to show him our appreciation. After all, we are in Babylon, not Israel. If only Daniel were here!"

It is easy to rationalize in situations far less intense than they were in, but they did not. Some things in life leave no room whatsoever for compromise—things like one's moral beliefs, and one's loyalty to God.

Where was Daniel? The Scripture simply does not say. However, we can be certain that, like his friends, Daniel would have refused to compromise and worship the image.

Daniel 3:13–18 — Three Hebrew Worthies Trust God

"Then Nebuchadnezzar, in rage and fury, gave the command to bring Shadrach, Meshach, and Abed-Nego. So they brought these men before the king. Nebuchadnezzar spoke, saying to them, 'Is it true, Shadrach, Meshach, and Abed-Nego, that you do not serve my gods or worship the gold image which I have set up? Now if you are ready at the time you hear the sound of the horn, flute, harp, lyre, and psaltery, in symphony with all kinds of music, and you fall down and worship the image which I have made, good! But if you do not worship, you shall be cast immediately into the midst of a burning fiery furnace. And who is the god who will deliver you from my hands?'

"Shadrach, Meshach, and Abed-Nego answered and said to the king, 'O Nebuchadnezzar, we have no need to answer you in this matter. If that is the case, our God whom we serve is able to deliver us from the burning fiery furnace, and He will deliver us from your hand, O king. But if not, let it be known to you, O king, that we do not serve your gods, nor will we worship the gold image which you have set up.'"

Consider This **Complete Trust**

Although this pagan king's temper seemed to have no limit, this time he went too far in challenging the God of heaven, saying, *"And who is the god who will deliver you from my hands?"* Daniel 3:15.

Little did Nebuchadnezzar then realize that he was but clay in the hands of the Potter. Before his life ended, he himself would bow down and worship—not before an image of gold, but before the King of the Universe.

In faith, the Hebrew men stood before the wrath and fury of the king! "Faith" is more than just "belief," a mental assent to truth, for *"Even the demons believe—and tremble!"* James 2:19. Scriptural faith also requires trust in God, and in His word. Throughout this great trial, Shadrach, Meshach, and Abed-Nego showed genuine faith. They told Nebuchadnezzar that their God was able to deliver them; but that even if He chose not to, they would continue to trust Him, and they would never worship the image!

Daniel 3:19–24 — God Protects Shadrach, Meshach, and Abed-Nego

"Then Nebuchadnezzar was full of fury, and the expression on his face changed toward Shadrach, Meshach, and Abed-Nego. He spoke and commanded that they heat the furnace seven times more than it was usually heated. And he commanded certain mighty men of valor who were in his army to bind Shadrach, Meshach, and Abed-Nego, and cast them into the burning fiery furnace. Then these men were bound in their coats, their trousers, their turbans, and their other garments, and were cast into the midst of the burning fiery furnace. Therefore, because the king's command was urgent, and the furnace exceedingly hot, the flame of the fire killed those men who took up Shadrach, Meshach, and Abed-Nego. And these three men, Shadrach, Meshach, and Abed-Nego, fell down bound into the midst of the burning fiery furnace.

"Then King Nebuchadnezzar was astonished; and he rose in haste and spoke, saying to his counselors, 'Did we not cast three men bound into the midst of the fire?'

"They answered and said to the king, 'True, O king.'"

Mighty to Save

Consider This

Whether closing the lions' mouths, or protecting the three young Hebrews from the fiery furnace, God is always present—carrying out His will and desire.

What a witness and testimony of the faithful, loving character of God! On Nebuchadnezzar's command, the furnace was heated seven times hotter than any inferno imaginable, even slaying the soldiers who threw the three Hebrews into the fire! Yet to his great amazement, the king saw not three men in the fire, but four, as the Lord God of the heat and cold walked among them!

Daniel 3:25 — The Son of God

"'Look!' he answered, 'I see four men loose, walking in the midst of the fire; and they are not hurt, and the form of the fourth is like the Son of God.'"

Preexistences of Jesus

Closer Look

Because of the prior witness of Daniel, this witness by his friends, and the glory of Christ's appearance in the furnace,

Nebuchadnezzar knew that this was indeed the Son of God!

This is not the first instance in the Old Testament Scriptures in which Christ revealed Himself. Previously, He had come to Abraham's tent (Genesis 18:1), followed Moses and the Israelites in the wilderness (1 Corinthians 10:1–4), and appeared to many of the prophets.

Jesus Himself said, *"Most assuredly, I say to you, before Abraham was, I Am."* John 8:58. *"And now, O Father, glorify Me together with Yourself, with the glory which I had with You before the world was."* John 17:5.

John the Baptist stated that Jesus existed before him. John 1:29–30.

Jesus is the Alpha and the Omega, the Beginning and the End. Revelation 22:13. He is the Great *"I AM"!* Exodus 3:14.

Daniel 3:26–30 — *Faithfulness Rewarded*

"Then Nebuchadnezzar went near the mouth of the burning fiery furnace and spoke, saying, Shadrach, Meshach, and Abed-Nego, servants of the Most High God, come out, and come here. Then Shadrach, Meshach, and Abed-Nego came from the midst of the fire. And the satraps, administrators, governors, and the king's counselors gathered together, and they saw these men on whose bodies the fire had no power; the hair of their head was not singed nor were their garments affected, and the smell of fire was not on them.

"Nebuchadnezzar spoke, saying, 'Blessed be the God of Shadrach, Meshach, and Abed-Nego, who sent His Angel and delivered His servants who trusted in Him, and they have frustrated the king's word, and yielded their bodies, that they should not serve nor worship any god except their own God! Therefore I make a decree that any people, nation, or language which speaks anything amiss against the God of Shadrach, Meshach, and Abed-Nego shall be cut in pieces, and their houses shall be made an ash heap; because there is no other God who can deliver like this.'

"Then the king promoted Shadrach, Meshach, and Abed-Nego in the province of Babylon."

Consider This

Not Even the Smell of Smoke

God honored these young men for their faithfulness to Him. Their hair was not singed. Their clothing was not scorched. They did not even smell of fire!

Their faithful witness affected the entire nation, causing Nebuchad-nezzar to realize that there was no other god like the God of Israel! However, the king had not yet been brought to the place where he was willing to accept the God of Israel as his God; that time was yet to come.

Shadrach, Meshach and Abed-Nego had shown that they were men of great integrity, the very type of men Nebuchadnezzar knew that he and his kingdom needed in positions of leadership.

DANIEL 4

1 Nebuchadnezzar the king, To all peoples, nations, and languages that dwell in all the earth:

Peace be multiplied to you.

2 I thought it good to declare the signs and wonders that the Most High God has worked for me.

3 How great are His signs, and how mighty His wonders! His kingdom is an everlasting kingdom, and His dominion is from generation to generation.

4 I, Nebuchadnezzar, was at rest in my house, and flourishing in my palace.

5 I saw a dream which made me afraid, and the thoughts on my bed and the visions of my head troubled me.

6 Therefore I issued a decree to bring in all the wise men of Babylon before me, that they might make known to me the interpretation of the dream.

7 Then the magicians, the astrologers, the Chaldeans, and the soothsayers came in, and I told them the dream; but they did not make known to me its interpretation.

8 But at last Daniel came before me (his name is Belteshazzar, according to the name of my god; in him is the Spirit of the Holy God), and I told the dream before him, saying:

9 "Belteshazzar, chief of the magicians, because I know that the Spirit of the Holy God is in you, and no secret troubles you, explain to me the visions of my dream that I have seen, and its interpretation.

10 "These were the visions of my head while on my bed: I was looking, and behold, a tree in the midst of the earth, and its height was great.

11 The tree grew and became strong; its height reached to the heavens, and it could be seen to the ends of all the earth.

12 Its leaves were lovely, Its fruit abundant,

And in it was food for all.

The beasts of the field found shade under it,

The birds of the heavens dwelt in its branches,

And all flesh was fed from it.

13 "I saw in the visions of my head while on my bed, and there was a watcher, a holy one, coming down from heaven.

14 He cried aloud and said thus: 'Chop down the tree and cut off its branches, strip off its leaves and scatter its fruit. Let the beasts get out from under it,

And the birds from its branches.

15 Nevertheless leave the stump and roots in the earth,

Bound with a band of iron and bronze,

In the tender grass of the field. Let it be wet with the dew of heaven,

And let him graze with the beasts On the grass of the earth.

16 Let his heart be changed from that of a man, let him be given the heart of a beast, and let seven times pass over him.

17 'This decision is by the decree of the watchers,

And the sentence by the word of the holy ones,

In order that the living may know that the Most High rules in the kingdom of men,

Gives it to whomever He will,

And sets over it the lowest of men.'

18 "This dream I, King Nebuchadnezzar, have seen. Now you, Belteshazzar, declare its interpretation, since all the wise men of my kingdom are not able to make known to me the interpretation; but you are able, for the Spirit of the Holy God is in you."

19 Then Daniel, whose name was Belteshazzar, was astonished for a time, and his thoughts troubled him. So the king spoke, and said, "Belteshazzar, do not let the dream or its interpretation trouble you." Belteshazzar answered and said, "My lord, may the dream concern those who hate you, and its interpretation concern your enemies!

20 "The tree that you saw, which grew and became strong, whose height reached to the heavens and which could be seen by all the earth,

21 whose leaves were lovely and its fruit abundant, in which was food for all, under which the beasts of the field dwelt, and in whose branches the birds of the heaven had their home—

22 it is you, O king, who have grown and become strong; for your greatness has grown and reaches to the heavens, and your dominion to the end of the earth.

23 "And inasmuch as the king saw a watcher, a holy one, coming down from heaven and saying, 'Chop down the tree and destroy it, but leave its stump and roots in the earth, bound with a band of iron and bronze in the tender grass of the field; let it be wet with the dew of heaven, and let him graze with the beasts of the field, till seven times pass over him';

24 this is the interpretation, O king, and this is the decree of the Most High, which has come upon my lord the king:

25 They shall drive you from men, your dwelling shall be with the beasts of the field, and they shall make you eat grass like oxen. They shall wet you with the dew of heaven, and seven times shall pass over you, till you know that the Most High rules in the kingdom of men, and gives it to whomever He chooses.

26 "And inasmuch as they gave the command to leave the stump and roots of the tree, your kingdom shall be assured to you, after you come to know that Heaven rules.

27 Therefore, O king, let my advice be acceptable to you; break off your sins by being righteous, and your iniquities by showing mercy to the poor. Perhaps there may be a lengthening of your prosperity."

28 All this came upon King Nebuchadnezzar.

29 At the end of the twelve months he was walking about the royal palace of Babylon.

30 The king spoke, saying, "Is not this great Babylon, that I have built for a royal dwelling by my mighty power and for the honor of my majesty?"

31 While the word was still in the king's mouth, a voice fell from heaven: "King Nebuchadnezzar, to you it is spoken: the kingdom has departed from you!

32 And they shall drive you from men, and your dwelling shall be with the beasts of the field. They shall make you eat grass like oxen; and seven times shall pass over you, until you know that the Most High rules in the kingdom of men, and gives it to whomever He chooses."

33 That very hour the word was fulfilled concerning Nebuchadnezzar; he was driven from men and ate grass like oxen; his body was wet with the dew of heaven till his hair had grown like eagles' feathers and his nails like birds' claws.

34 And at the end of the time I, Nebuchadnezzar, lifted my eyes to heaven, and my understanding returned to me; and I blessed the Most High and praised and honored Him who lives forever: For His dominion is an everlasting dominion, and His kingdom is from generation to generation.

35 All the inhabitants of the earth are reputed as nothing; He does according to His will in the army of heaven and among the inhabitants of the earth. No one can restrain His hand or go say to Him, "What have You done?"

36 At the same time my reason returned to me, and for the glory of my kingdom, my honor and splendor returned to me. My counselors and nobles resorted to me, I was restored to my kingdom, and excellent majesty was added to me.

37 Now I, Nebuchadnezzar, praise and extol and honor the King of heaven, all of whose works are truth, and His ways justice. And those who walk in pride He is able to put down.

CHAPTER 4

Nebuchadnezzar's Conversion

Inside this Chapter

Daniel 4:1–3 — Nebuchadnezzar's Proclamation

"Nebuchadnezzar the king, To all peoples, nations, and languages that dwell in all the earth: Peace be multiplied to you. I thought it good to declare the signs and wonders that the Most High God has worked for me. How great are His signs, and how mighty His wonders! His kingdom is an everlasting kingdom, and His dominion is from generation to generation."

Consider This

Written by Nebuchadnezzar

Nebuchadnezzar himself wrote this chapter. In it, he tells of the greatness of God's kingdom, and of his own humiliation and conversion. No other chapter in the Bible tells so plainly how a nation's strength and prosperity are determined by its faithfulness in fulfilling God's purpose.

Daniel 4:4–7 — Nebuchadnezzar's Vision

"I, Nebuchadnezzar, was at rest in my house, and flourishing in my palace. I saw a dream which made me afraid, and the thoughts on my bed and the visions of my head troubled me. Therefore I issued a decree to bring in all the wise men of Babylon before me, that they might make known to me the interpretation of the dream. Then the magicians, the astrologers, the Chaldeans, and the soothsayers came in, and I told them the dream; but they did not make known to me its interpretation."

Consider This

Greatest Ruler of the Age

As the years passed, Nebuchadnezzar lost sight of the warnings and instruction God had previously given him. He should have learned from his prior dream experience to trust in the God of Heaven rather than in Babylon's wise men, yet once again, he initially seeks their counsel!

Nebuchadnezzar had changed his focus to building and strengthening his kingdom. Tyre and Egypt fell prey to his conquest. Babylon, which was called "The Golden City," increased Nebuchadnezzar's fame, making him the greatest ruler of the age. In His mercy, God gave the king another dream, attempting to save him from claiming for himself the glory that belongs only to the Creator, and to the Supreme Ruler.

Daniel 4:8–9 — Daniel Called

"But at last Daniel came before me (his name is Belteshazzar, according to the name of my god; in him is the Spirit of the Holy God), and I told the dream before him, saying: 'Belteshazzar, chief of the magicians, because I know that the Spirit of the Holy God is in you, and no secret troubles you, explain to me the visions of my dream that I have seen, and its interpretation.'"

Closer Look

Interpreter of Dreams

In the early part of Nebuchadnezzar's reign, Daniel brought relief to the king's troubled mind by recounting for him his forgotten dream, and then interpreting his dream for him.

Now, God has given Nebuchadnezzar another perplexing dream, but this time the king remembers what he dreamed. He foolishly shares the details of his dream with the wise men, asking them only for the dream's interpretation—yet they cannot even accomplish that! The king finally does what he should have learned to do before, and summons Daniel to tell him the dream's meaning.

Daniel 4:10–18 — The Great Tree

"These were the visions of my head while on my bed: I was looking, and behold, a tree in the midst of the earth, and its height was great. The tree grew and became strong; its height reached to the heavens, and it could be seen to the ends of all the earth. Its leaves were lovely, its fruit abundant, and in it was food for all. The beasts of the field found shade under it, the birds of the heavens dwelt in its branches, and all flesh was fed from it.

"I saw in the visions of my head while on my bed, and there was a watcher, a holy one, coming down from heaven. He cried aloud and said thus: 'Chop down the tree and cut off its branches, strip off its leaves and scatter its fruit. Let the beasts get out from under it, and the birds from its branches. Nevertheless leave the stump and roots in the earth, bound with a band of iron and bronze, in the tender grass of the field. Let it be wet with the dew of heaven, and let him graze with the beasts on the grass of the earth. Let his heart be changed from that of a man, let him be given the heart of a beast, And let seven times pass over him. This decision is by the decree of the watchers, and the sentence by the word of the holy ones, in order that

the living may know that the Most High rules in the kingdom of men, gives it to whomever He will, and sets over it the lowest of men.'

"This dream I, King Nebuchadnezzar, have seen. Now you, Belteshazzar, declare its interpretation, since all the wise men of my kingdom are not able to make known to me the interpretation; but you are able, for the Spirit of the Holy God is in you."

Closer Look — Nebuchadnezzar's Dream

Nebuchadnezzar had reached the pinnacle of his reign. Ezekiel the prophet referred to him as the *"king of kings"* (Ezekiel 26:7), and as the *"terrible of the nations"* (Ezekiel 28:7). Babylon, *"the golden city"* (Isaiah 14:4), became *"the praise of the whole earth"* (Jeremiah 51:41). It was one of the wonders of the world, with walls and gates of magnificent size and height. Its hanging gardens were called one of the Seven Wonders of the World. Nebuchadnezzar described his monumental rebuilding of the city of Babylon as follows: *"My name will be remembered throughout history for all time because I turned Babylon and Esagila into a mighty fortress"* (from an East India Tablet). Proud and haughty, he believed his kingdom reached to the ends of the earth.

As a result, God used a tree, seen from the ends of the earth and whose top reached to heaven, to represent the kingdom of Babylon. Its leaves provided shelter, and its fruit provided food for all humanity. By cutting the tree down rather than uprooting it, and by leaving the stump with bands around it, God showed that the kingdom of Babylon would continue. He used the bands of iron and bronze to illustrate that Babylon's influence would continue into the subsequent kingdoms of Greece and Rome, which those two metals represented in the great image of Daniel 2. In fact, the stump and roots of the tree point to the enduring influence of the Babylonian government until the end of time. That is why the book of Revelation states, *"Come out of her [Babylon], My people..."* Revelation 18:4.

In His great plan, God has assigned a place to every nation and individual. The *"Watcher and Holy One"* is looking to see if we are fulfilling His purpose for our lives. By our own choices, each one of us decides our own destiny. Still, God has the power to counteract our wrong choices for the accomplishment of His ultimate purpose.

Daniel 4:19–27 — *Daniel Interprets the Dream*

"*Then Daniel, whose name was Belteshazzar, was astonished for a time, and his thoughts troubled him. So the king spoke, and said, 'Belteshazzar, do not let the dream or its interpretation trouble you.' Belteshazzar answered and said, 'My lord, may the dream concern those who hate you, and its interpretation concern your enemies!*

"'*The tree that you saw, which grew and became strong, whose height reached to the heavens and which could be seen by all the earth, whose leaves were lovely and its fruit abundant, in which was food for all, under which the beasts of the field dwelt, and in whose branches the birds of the heaven had their home—it is you, O king, who have grown and become strong; for your greatness has grown and reaches to the heavens, and your dominion to the end of the earth.*

"*And inasmuch as the king saw a watcher, a holy one, coming down from heaven and saying, "Chop down the tree and destroy it, but leave its stump and roots in the earth, bound with a band of iron and bronze in the tender grass of the field; let it be wet with the dew of heaven, and let him graze with the beasts of the field, till seven times pass over him"; this is the interpretation, O king, and this is the decree of the Most High, which has come upon my lord the king: They shall drive you from men, your dwelling shall be with the beasts of the field, and they shall make you eat grass like oxen. They shall wet you with the dew of heaven, and seven times shall pass over you, till you know that the Most High rules in the kingdom of men, and gives it to whomever He chooses.*

"*And inasmuch as they gave the command to leave the stump and roots of the tree, your kingdom shall be assured to you, after you come to know that Heaven rules. Therefore, O king, let my advice be acceptable to you; break off your sins by being righteous, and your iniquities by showing mercy to the poor. Perhaps there may be a lengthening of your prosperity.*'"

The Most High Rules

Since the kingdom of Babylon lasted only seventy years, and Nebuchadnezzar ruled for forty of them, this dream referred not only to him, but also to the kingdom as a whole. Seven times in this chapter alone, it affirms that God is the One who rules, who sets up kings and takes them down. In His mercy, God warned the king to humbly accept the fact that all he had accomplished was by the blessing of God. If he did not, he would eat grass like an ox until "seven times" passed over him. The word "times" in Aramaic is *iddan*, meaning "years."

God's promises, good or bad, are always conditional. This concept is very important in understanding Bible prophecy. By the decree of the Most High, Nebuchadnezzar received a time of probation in which to recognize that the God of Daniel ruled in the affairs of all humanity.

🔍 *Daniel 4:28–30* — The City of Babylon

"All this came upon King Nebuchadnezzar. At the end of the twelve months he was walking about the royal palace of Babylon. The king spoke, saying, 'Is not this great Babylon, that I have built for a royal dwelling by my mighty power and for the honor of my majesty?'"

Babylon the Great

Babylon was an old city, dating back to the time of Nimrod, its original builder (Genesis 10:10). The word *"Babel"* is the Hebrew word for Babylon. It was already a flourishing city when Abraham (Abram) left southern Mesopotamia in around 2,000 B.C. Genesis 11:31. The ruins of Babylon lie on the Euphrates River, in the country of Iraq, about 50 miles south of Baghdad.

Babylon became the capital of the Neo-Babylonian Empire in 605 B.C., when Nabopolassar took over the Assyrian Empire. However, it was under King Nebuchadnezzar that Babylon reached the height of its splendor. He enlarged the city to an area approximately 13 miles long by 10 miles wide. Surrounding the city he built a double wall approximately 50 feet thick. It had 250 towers, and eight gates. The most famous was the Ishtar Gate, which opened upon a sacred processional way leading to the temple of the pagan god, Marduk.

This gate, and the city walls, were decorated with yellow, green and red glazed bricks, which featured drawings of lions, dragons, and bulls on a blue background.

The center of Babylon's glory was its famous temple, Etemenanki, which was 300 feet square at its base, and over 300 feet high.

Another of Nebuchadnezzar's achievements was the hanging gardens he built for his wife. Since Babylon was located on the plains and his wife was from a mountainous area, the gardens served to remind her of her mountain home. The Hanging Gardens of Babylon were so beautiful that they became known as one of the Seven Wonders of the Ancient World.

In the northwest corner of the inner city stood the Southern Palace, which served as the official residence of the king. All the state ceremonies took place there, and at its center stood the throne room—173 feet long, 57 feet wide, and 66 feet high! This immense hall was most likely where Belshazzar's feast took place years later, and where the handwriting on the wall appeared (Daniel 5:5).

Nebuchadnezzar wanted the city of Babylon to last forever. Archaeologists have found bricks with the inscription: "The city which is the delight of my eyes, may it last forever." However, God prophesied otherwise.

Daniel 4:31–33 — Nebuchadnezzar's Humiliation

"While the word was still in the king's mouth, a voice fell from heaven: 'King Nebuchadnezzar, to you it is spoken: the kingdom has departed from you! And they shall drive you from men, and your dwelling shall be with the beasts of the field. They shall make you eat grass like oxen; and seven times shall pass over you, until you know that the Most High rules in the kingdom of men, and gives it to whomever He chooses.

"That very hour the word was fulfilled concerning Nebuchadnezzar; he was driven from men and ate grass like oxen; his body was wet with the dew of heaven till his hair had grown like eagles' feathers and his nails like birds' claws."

Consider This

Eating Grass Like Oxen

As the words came from Neduchadnezzar's lips, the tree fell, and his ability to reason departed. He who once believed his great ability had built the kingdom was suddenly no longer capable of carrying on an intelligent conversation. God reduced the proud monarch's actions to that of a beast. For fully seven years he would be humiliated before the nations, dwelling with the cattle, and eating grass as his daily food. However, God saw in the king a changeable heart (1 Samuel 16:7). Nebuchadnezzar's punishment was severe, but sometimes God must use tough love to get a person's attention, in order to lead him to salvation.

Daniel 4:34–37 — *Nebuchadnezzar's Conversion*

"And at the end of the time I, Nebuchadnezzar, lifted my eyes to heaven, and my understanding returned to me; and I blessed the Most High and praised and honored Him who lives forever: For His dominion is an everlasting dominion, and His kingdom is from generation to generation. All the inhabitants of the earth are reputed as nothing; He does according to His will in the army of heaven and among the inhabitants of the earth. No one can restrain His hand or say to Him, 'What have You done?'

"At the same time my reason returned to me, and for the glory of my kingdom, my honor and splendor returned to me. My counselors and nobles resorted to me, I was restored to my kingdom, and excellent majesty was added to me. Now I, Nebuchadnezzar, praise and extol and honor the King of heaven, all of whose works are truth, and His ways justice. And those who walk in pride He is able to put down.

Nebuchadnezzar's Public Proclamation

The proud, tyrannical and overbearing king became a humble child of God, and a compassionate ruler. Nebuchadnezzar had finally accepted the wisdom in the divine hand of God, whose chastening was necessary to bring about the change of his heart, and the transformation of his character.

In His mercy, God restored the kingdom to Nebuchadnezzar, who became a witness of the grace and righteousness of the King of Heaven for the rest of his life.

DANIEL 5

1 Belshazzar the king made a great feast for a thousand of his lords, and drank wine in the presence of the thousand.

2 While he tasted the wine, Belshazzar gave the command to bring the gold and silver vessels which his father Nebuchadnezzar had taken from the temple which had been in Jerusalem, that the king and his lords, his wives, and his concubines might drink from them.

3 Then they brought the gold vessels that had been taken from the temple of the house of God which had been in Jerusalem; and the king and his lords, his wives, and his concubines drank from them.

4 They drank wine, and praised the gods of gold and silver, bronze and iron, wood and stone.

5 In the same hour the fingers of a man's hand appeared and wrote opposite the lampstand on the plaster of the wall of the king's palace; and the king saw the part of the hand that wrote.

6 Then the king's countenance changed, and his thoughts troubled him, so that the joints of his hips were loosened and his knees knocked against each other.

7 The king cried aloud to bring in the astrologers, the Chaldeans, and the soothsayers. The king spoke, saying to the wise men of Babylon, "Whoever reads this writing, and tells me its interpretation, shall be clothed with purple and have a chain of gold around his neck; and he shall be the third ruler in the kingdom."

8 Now all the king's wise men came, but they could not read the writing, or make known to the king its interpretation.

9 Then King Belshazzar was greatly troubled, his countenance was changed, and his lords were astonished.

10 The queen, because of the words of the king and his lords, came to the banquet hall. The queen spoke, saying, "O king, live forever! Do not let your thoughts trouble you, nor let your countenance change.

11 There is a man in your kingdom in whom is the Spirit of the Holy God. And in the days of your father, light and understanding and wisdom, like the wisdom of the gods, were found in him; and King Nebuchadnezzar your father—your father the king—made him chief of the magicians, astrologers, Chaldeans, and soothsayers.

12 Inasmuch as an excellent spirit, knowledge, understanding,

interpreting dreams, solving riddles, and explaining enigmas were found in this Daniel, whom the king named Belteshazzar, now let Daniel be called, and he will give the interpretation."

13 Then Daniel was brought in before the king. The king spoke, and said to Daniel, "Are you that Daniel who is one of the captives from Judah, whom my father the king brought from Judah?

14 I have heard of you, that the Spirit of God is in you, and that light and understanding and excellent wisdom are found in you.

15 Now the wise men, the astrologers, have been brought in before me, that they should read this writing and make known to me its interpretation, but they could not give the interpretation of the thing.

16 And I have heard of you, that you can give interpretations and explain enigmas. Now if you can read the writing and make known to me its interpretation, you shall be clothed with purple and have a chain of gold around your neck, and shall be the third ruler in the kingdom."

17 Then Daniel answered, and said before the king, "Let your gifts be for yourself, and give your rewards to another; yet I will read the writing to the king, and make known to him the interpretation.

18 O king, the Most High God gave Nebuchadnezzar your father a kingdom and majesty, glory and honor.

19 And because of the majesty that He gave him, all peoples, nations, and languages trembled and feared before him. Whomever he wished, he executed; whomever he wished, he kept alive; whomever he wished, he set up; and whomever he wished, he put down.

20 But when his heart was lifted up, and his spirit was hardened in pride, he was deposed from his kingly throne, and they took his glory from him.

21 Then he was driven from the sons of men, his heart was made like the beasts, and his dwelling was with the wild donkeys. They fed him with grass like oxen, and his body was wet with the dew of heaven, till he knew that the Most High God rules in the kingdom of men, and appoints over it whomever He chooses.

22 "But you his son, Belshazzar, have not humbled your heart, although you knew all this.

23 And you have lifted yourself up against the Lord of heaven. They have brought the vessels of His house before you, and you and your lords, your wives and your concubines, have drunk wine from them. And you have praised the gods of silver and gold, bronze and iron, wood and stone, which do not see or hear or know; and the

God who holds your breath in His hand and owns all your ways, you have not glorified.

24 Then the fingers of the hand were sent from Him, and this writing was written.

25 "And this is the inscription that was written: MENE, MENE, TEKEL, UPHARSIN.

26 This is the interpretation of each word. MENE: God has numbered your kingdom, and finished it;

27 TEKEL: You have been weighed in the balances, and found wanting;

28 PERES: Your kingdom has been divided, and given to the Medes and Persians."

29 Then Belshazzar gave the command, and they clothed Daniel with purple and put a chain of gold around his neck, and made a proclamation concerning him that he should be the third ruler in the kingdom.

30 That very night Belshazzar, king of the Chaldeans, was slain.

31 And Darius the Mede received the kingdom, being about sixty-two years old.

CHAPTER 5

The Fall of Babylon

Inside this Chapter

Daniel 5:1–2 — Belshazzar's Contempt of God

"Belshazzar the king made a great feast for a thousand of his lords, and drank wine in the presence of the thousand. While he tasted the wine, Belshazzar gave the command to bring the gold and silver vessels which his father Nebuchadnezzar had taken from the temple which had been in Jerusalem, that the king and his lords, his wives, and his concubines might drink from them."

Closer Look — *The Young King*

In the Bible, the term "father" can refer to a person's father or grandfather. Belshazzar's father was Nabonidus, Nebuchadnezzar's son; therefore, Belshazzar was Nebuchadnezzar's grandson.

Nabonidus did not like being king; in fact, he hated it. He preferred to live in an oasis in the Arabian Desert called, "The Oasis of Teman." According to his own chronicles, he transferred power to his 15-year old son, Belshazzar, in 553 B.C., and then left to enjoy himself at his summer home in Teman. Thirteen years later, on October 12, 539 B.C., Belshazzar held an autumn festival. During the festival, he brought out the sacred vessels his grandfather Nebuchadnezzar had brought from Solomon's temple in Jerusalem, after he had destroyed it.

Daniel 5:3–4 — Sacred Vessels

"Then they brought the gold vessels that had been taken from the temple of the house of God which had been in Jerusalem; and the king and his lords, his wives, and his concubines drank from them. They drank wine, and praised the gods of gold and silver, bronze and iron, wood and stone."

Consider This — *Drunk and Out of Control*

Those sacred vessels had been dedicated to the Lord, and were only to be used in the Sanctuary services. They were to receive the utmost respect and reverence, and even Nebuchadnezzar treated them with esteem.

Intoxicated with wine, his reason dethroned, and with lust and passion in control, young king Belshazzar called for the sacred vessels and used them in their drunken feast to worship their pagan gods of silver and gold.

Belshazzar knew better. Without a doubt, the conversion of his grandfather, the witness of Daniel and his friends, and the stories of God's leading had been shared with him. Suddenly, in the midst of this insulting sacrilege, the God of Israel brought down the curtain on the kingdom of Babylon.

Daniel 5:5–9 — Handwriting Terrifies the King

"In the same hour the fingers of a man's hand appeared and wrote opposite the lampstand on the plaster of the wall of the king's palace; and the king saw the part of the hand that wrote. Then the king's countenance changed, and his thoughts troubled him, so that the joints of his hips were loosened and his knees knocked against each other. The king cried aloud to bring in the astrologers, the Chaldeans, and the soothsayers. The king spoke, saying to the wise men of Babylon, 'Whoever reads this writing, and tells me its interpretation, shall be clothed with purple and have a chain of gold around his neck; and he shall be the third ruler in the kingdom.' Now all the king's wise men came, but they could not read the writing, or make known to the king its interpretation. Then King Belshazzar was greatly troubled, his countenance was changed, and his lords were astonished."

Consider This

The Bloodless Hand

At the height of the feast, the boisterous mirth was hushed. The crowd began to shake with indescribable terror as their eyes fastened upon the bloodless hand writing burning words upon the plaster wall. Each letter formed like lightning, and then lingered with awesome and terrible significance.

Belshazzar was the most shocked and frightened of all. His entire being trembled as he called for his counselors to come and explain the mystery. He offered them great rewards for the answer, but the wisdom of heaven cannot be bought or sold.

Daniel 5:10–12 — The Queen Mother

"The queen, because of the words of the king and his lords, came to the banquet hall. The queen spoke, saying, 'O king, live forever! Do not let your thoughts trouble you, nor let your countenance change. There is a man in your kingdom in whom is the Spirit of the Holy God. And in the days of your father, light and understanding and wisdom, like the wisdom of the gods,

were found in him; and King Nebuchadnezzar your father—your father the king—made him chief of the magicians, astrologers, Chaldeans, and soothsayers. Inasmuch as an excellent spirit, knowledge, understanding, interpreting dreams, solving riddles, and explaining enigmas were found in this Daniel, whom the king named Belteshazzar, now let Daniel be called, and he will give the interpretation.'"

Old but Not Forgotten

(Closer Look) The queen mentioned here is without a doubt the mother of Belshazzar. Archeologists have discovered that Belshazzar's grandmother died in 547 B.C., and according to Oriental custom, none but a ruling monarch's mother would dare enter a king's presence without being summoned. As a child, she had seen and heard many of the events in which Daniel and her father, Nebuchadnezzar, had been involved.

After God restored Nebuchadnezzar's memory and kingdom, he lived only a few more years. A new regime then came into power as his son and grandson, Nabonidus and Belshazzar, ruled together. That is why Belshazzar said that the person who could decipher the handwriting would be made *"third"* in the kingdom.

The policy of righteousness and justice that Daniel stood for came into disfavor, and he was retired from public service. The fact that Daniel later entered the service of Persia shows that his retirement at the close of the Babylonian Empire was not due to old age, or to ill health.

Now, as Belshazzar faced the crisis of the handwriting on the wall, and the inability of his wise men to interpret it, the queen mother clearly remembered Daniel, and his wise counsel to King Nebuchadnezzar. Daniel's candid reprimand of Belshazzar's lifestyle and policies showed his disapproval of how the current affairs of state were being handled.

Daniel 5:13–24 — Daniel Brought Before the King

"Then Daniel was brought in before the king. The king spoke, and said to Daniel, 'Are you that Daniel who is one of the captives from Judah, whom my father the king brought from Judah? I have heard of you, that the Spirit of God is in you, and that light and understanding and excellent wisdom are found in you. Now the wise men, the astrologers, have been brought in before me, that they should read this writing and make known to me its interpretation, but they could not give the interpretation of the thing. And

I have heard of you, that you can give interpretations and explain enigmas. Now if you can read the writing and make known to me its interpretation, you shall be clothed with purple and have a chain of gold around your neck, and shall be the third ruler in the kingdom.'

'Then Daniel answered, and said before the king, 'Let your gifts be for yourself, and give your rewards to another; yet I will read the writing to the king, and make known to him the interpretation. O king, the Most High God gave Nebuchadnezzar your father a kingdom and majesty, glory and honor. And because of the majesty that He gave him, all peoples, nations, and languages trembled and feared before him. Whomever he wished, he executed; whomever he wished, he kept alive; whomever he wished, he set up; and whomever he wished, he put down. But when his heart was lifted up, and his spirit was hardened in pride, he was deposed from his kingly throne, and they took his glory from him. Then he was driven from the sons of men, his heart was made like the beasts, and his dwelling was with the wild donkeys. They fed him with grass like oxen, and his body was wet with the dew of heaven, till he knew that the Most High God rules in the kingdom of men, and appoints over it whomever He chooses.*

"'But you his son, Belshazzar, have not humbled your heart, although you knew all this. And you have lifted yourself up against the Lord of heaven. They have brought the vessels of His house before you, and you and your lords, your wives and your concubines, have drunk wine from them. And you have praised the gods of silver and gold, bronze and iron, wood and stone, which do not see or hear or know; and the God who holds your breath in His hand and owns all your ways, you have not glorified. Then the fingers of the hand were sent from Him, and this writing was written.'"

Consider This — *Wasted Opportunities*

Belshazzar had wasted the opportunities God had graciously granted him. His love of amusement and self-glorification erased the instruction he should never have forgotten. Daniel plainly told the king that God's judgment upon Babylon was the result of his disregard of Heaven-sent light. This is a lesson to us all—we are responsible for what we know.

Daniel 5:25–29 — *Mene, Mene, Tekel, Upharsin*

"And this is the inscription that was written: MENE, MENE, TEKEL,

UPHARSIN. *This is the interpretation of each word. MENE: God has numbered your kingdom, and finished it; TEKEL: You have been weighed in the balances, and found wanting; PERES: Your kingdom has been divided, and given to the Medes and Persians.' Then Belshazzar gave the command, and they clothed Daniel with purple and put a chain of gold around his neck, and made a proclamation concerning him that he should be the third ruler in the kingdom."*

Handwriting on the Wall

Consider This
Belshazzar and the wise men could read the handwriting on the wall, but they could not understand its meaning. They summoned Daniel because of his proven ability to interpret dreams and enigmas. The style of the handwriting on the wall made it a puzzle:

Mene—weighed; Tekel—balance; Peres—broken (the actual form of the last word—Peres—is UPHA RSIN, the ancient Aramaic word for PERSIA).

Daniel 5:30 — *Belshazzar is Slain*

"That very night Belshazzar, king of the Chaldeans, was slain."

The Euphrates Dries Up

Closer Look
According to the ancient historian Herodotus, Cyrus of Medo-Persia entered Babylon by drying up the Euphrates river.

Centuries before the time of Cyrus, an Assyrian queen of Nineveh built a summer palace upstream from Babylon. She had slaves hollow out a man-made lake there, which was fed by waters from the Euphrates River. When she died, her dynasty was replaced, and her summer palace and private lake were forgotten. As a result, the lake dried up in disrepair.

Cyrus had his engineers dig a channel from the Euphrates River to that old lakebed, diverting the waters of the Euphrates, and causing it to dry up downstream. He then entered Babylon through the gates that allowed the Euphrates to flow through the city, just as the Scriptures had predicted in Isaiah 45:1. That very night, Belshazzar was slain, and the Babylonian Empire came to its end.

Daniel 5:31 — Medes and Persians Overthrow Babylon

"And Darius the Mede received the kingdom, being about sixty-two years old."

Cyrus in Prophecy

With the death of Darius two years later, Cyrus became king. Daniel continued his service in the courts of Medo-Persia until the first year of Cyrus' reign. Babylon fell to the Medo-Persians—exactly as Daniel had prophesied 50 years before Cyrus was born (see chapter 2). Daniel had no-doubt shown Cyrus the Scripture which mentioned him by name (Isaiah 45), and that very likely made an impact on him (see Ezra 1:1–4), influencing him to decree that the children of Israel should return to Jerusalem, and rebuild the temple.

Cyrus lived a charmed life. The magi told his grandfather, Astyages, that Cyrus would one day take over his kingdom. Because of this, Astyages made several failed attempts on Cyrus' life.

The fifth chapter of Daniel is also very important because John refers to it—and the events surrounding it—in Revelation 16:12, *"Then the sixth angel poured out his bowl on the great river Euphrates, and its water was dried up, so that the way of the kings from the east might be prepared."* This is a direct reference to the story of how Cyrus diverted the Euphrates River, as detailed by Herodotus. According to Isaiah 44:28–45:1, Cyrus was an "anointed" or "messianic" figure who would come from the east, and allow God's people to return to Judah and Jerusalem. Cyrus did prefigure the work of Jesus as Messiah, for Revelation 16:12 refers to Messiah Jesus as a king coming from the east to set us free.

NKJV

DANIEL 6

1 It pleased Darius to set over the kingdom one hundred and twenty satraps, to be over the whole kingdom;

2 and over these, three governors, of whom Daniel was one, that the satraps might give account to them, so that the king would suffer no loss.

3 Then this Daniel distinguished himself above the governors and satraps, because an excellent spirit was in him; and the king gave thought to setting him over the whole realm.

4 So the governors and satraps sought to find some charge against Daniel concerning the kingdom; but they could find no charge or fault, because he was faithful; nor was there any error or fault found in him.

5 Then these men said, "We shall not find any charge against this Daniel unless we find it against him concerning the law of his God."

6 So these governors and satraps thronged before the king, and said thus to him: "King Darius, live forever!

7 All the governors of the kingdom, the administrators and satraps, the counselors and advisors, have consulted together to establish a royal statute and to make a firm decree, that whoever petitions any god or man for thirty days, except you, O king, shall be cast into the den of lions.

8 Now, O king, establish the decree and sign the writing, so that it cannot be changed, according to the law of the Medes and Persians, which does not alter."

9 Therefore King Darius signed the written decree.

10 Now when Daniel knew that the writing was signed, he went home. And in his upper room, with his windows open toward Jerusalem, he knelt down on his knees three times that day, and prayed and gave thanks before his God, as was his custom since early days.

11 Then these men assembled and found Daniel praying and making supplication before his God.

12 And they went before the king, and spoke concerning the king's decree: "Have you not signed a decree that every man who petitions any god or man within thirty days, except you, O king, shall be cast into the den of lions?" The king answered and said, "The thing is true, according to the law of the Medes and Persians, which

does not alter."

13 So they answered and said before the king, "That Daniel, who is one of the captives from Judah, does not show due regard for you, O king, or for the decree that you have signed, but makes his petition three times a day."

14 And the king, when he heard these words, was greatly displeased with himself, and set his heart on Daniel to deliver him; and he labored till the going down of the sun to deliver him.

15 Then these men approached the king, and said to the king, "Know, O king, that it is the law of the Medes and Persians that no decree or statute which the king establishes may be changed."

16 So the king gave the command, and they brought Daniel and cast him into the den of lions. But the king spoke, saying to Daniel, "Your God, whom you serve continually, He will deliver you."

17 Then a stone was brought and laid on the mouth of the den, and the king sealed it with his own signet ring and with the signets of his lords, that the purpose concerning Daniel might not be changed.

18 Now the king went to his palace and spent the night fasting; and no musicians were brought before him. Also his sleep went from him.

19 Then the king arose very early in the morning and went in haste to the den of lions.

20 And when he came to the den, he cried out with a lamenting voice to Daniel. The king spoke, saying to Daniel, "Daniel, servant of the living God, has your God, whom you serve continually, been able to deliver you from the lions?"

21 Then Daniel said to the king, "O king, live forever!

22 My God sent His angel and shut the lions' mouths, so that they have not hurt me, because I was found innocent before Him; and also, O king, I have done no wrong before you."

23 Now the king was exceedingly glad for him, and commanded that they should take Daniel up out of the den. So Daniel was taken up out of the den, and no injury whatever was found on him, because he believed in his God.

24 And the king gave the command, and they brought those men who had accused Daniel, and they cast them into the den of lions — them, their children, and their wives; and the lions overpowered them, and broke all their bones in pieces before they ever came to the bottom of the den.

25 Then King Darius wrote:
To all peoples, nations, and languages that dwell in all the earth:
Peace be multiplied to you.

26 I make a decree that in every dominion of my kingdom men must tremble and fear before the God of Daniel.
For He is the living God,
And steadfast forever;
His kingdom is the one which shall not be destroyed,
And His dominion shall endure to the end.

27 He delivers and rescues,
And He works signs and wonders
In heaven and on earth,
Who has delivered Daniel from
the power of the lions.
28 So this Daniel prospered in the reign of Darius and in the reign of Cyrus the Persian.

CHAPTER 6

Daniel in the Lions' Den

Inside this Chapter

Daniel 6:1–2 — Daniel Prime Minister Again

"It pleased Darius to set over the kingdom one hundred and twenty satraps, to be over the whole kingdom; and over these, three governors, of whom Daniel was one, that the satraps might give account to them, so that the king would suffer no loss."

Consider This

Reorganization

The word "satrap" is similar to our word for "prince." As has been true throughout history, new leadership brings new organization. This story takes an unusual turn, however, when Daniel is appointed one of the three governors over the 120 princes. In the preceding chapter, we found Daniel to be third in order in the rule of Babylon.

It was unheard of for the prime minister of a conquered nation to then become a prime minister of the nation that had overthrown it. In most cases, the victorious nation put all the leaders of the defeated nation to death. However, Daniel's reputation preceded him, for the fact that he was prime minister of Babylon placed him in contact with leaders of other nations. Darius was fully convinced that Daniel was an utterly capable, and trustworthy, man.

Daniel 6:3 — Daniel's Excellent Spirit

"Then this Daniel distinguished himself above the governors and satraps, because an excellent spirit was in him; and the king gave thought to setting him over the whole realm."

Closer Look

A Class by Himself

This was not the first time Daniel's excellent spirit was revealed. Nebuchadnezzar observed it (Daniel 4:8), and the queen mother referred to the same quality in him (Daniel 5:11–12). Daniel was unwavering in faithfulness, loyal to duty, and showed unquestionable integrity in his words and actions. He was a noble statesman, but not a politician—qualities not often seen in public servants of his day, or ours.

If they are true to Him, the Lord is pleased to have intelligent men and women in business, and in public office. Daniel's example proves that, even in today's world, a person does not need to be dishonest or conniving in their dealings in order to succeed. No matter what the circumstances are, we can maintain our integrity by trusting the Lord.

Daniel 6:4–9 — A Foolish Decree

"So the governors and satraps sought to find some charge against Daniel concerning the kingdom; but they could find no charge or fault, because he was faithful; nor was there any error or fault found in him. Then these men said, 'We shall not find any charge against this Daniel unless we find it against him concerning the law of his God.'

"So these governors and satraps thronged before the king, and said thus to him: 'King Darius, live forever! All the governors of the kingdom, the administrators and satraps, the counselors and advisors, have consulted together to establish a royal statute and to make a firm decree, that whoever petitions any god or man for thirty days, except you, O king, shall be cast into the den of lions. Now, O king, establish the decree and sign the writing, so that it cannot be changed, according to the law of the Medes and Persians, which does not alter.' Therefore King Darius signed the written decree."

Consider This **Thorn in the Flesh**
It has been said that the honesty of a man is like a thorn in the flesh to the unjust. Yet how could the unjust princes succeed in condemning Daniel, who was faithful and true in all things?

The satraps were most careful to ensure that their motives went undetected; and, when nothing else worked, flattery did. The princes told Darius that the kingdom needed to be made aware of the power and majesty of its new king. Therefore, they proposed that the people should bring their petitions only to him, and not to any other man or god, for thirty days.

For 68 years, Daniel had given God top priority in his life. The governors and princes well-knew that he would not conform to their petition. However, Darius was carried away by the attention and praise, unaware of the underlying motive of the decree he was signing.

Daniel 6:10–11 — Daniel's Lifestyle Unchanged

"Now when Daniel knew that the writing was signed, he went home. And

in his upper room, with his windows open toward Jerusalem, he knelt down on his knees three times that day, and prayed and gave thanks before his God, as was his custom since early days.

"Then these men assembled and found Daniel praying and making supplication before his God."

New Circumstances

Consider This

God does not ask us to handle the circumstances of our lives. He only asks us to commit our lives to Him, and trust Him to handle the rest. Faith means simply resting in God's care.

Daniel knew about the signing of the decree, but it made no difference in his daily life. He continued his custom of praying three times a day—his living connection with Heaven. To sever his communion with his Lord would be as painful to him as depriving himself of breath.

Faith makes a person's witness consistent with his or her belief, and Daniel's witness was living proof that he trusted God to take care of all circumstances, regardless of the outcome.

Daniel 6:12–15 — Daniel Accused

"And they went before the king, and spoke concerning the king's decree: 'Have you not signed a decree that every man who petitions any god or man within thirty days, except you, O king, shall be cast into the den of lions?'

"The king answered and said, 'The thing is true, according to the law of the Medes and Persians, which does not alter.'

"So they answered and said before the king, 'That Daniel, who is one of the captives from Judah, does not show due regard for you, O king, or for the decree that you have signed, but makes his petition three times a day.'

"And the king, when he heard these words, was greatly displeased with himself, and set his heart on Daniel to deliver him; and he labored till the going down of the sun to deliver him. Then these men approached the king, and said to the king, 'Know, O king, that it is the law of the Medes and Persians that no decree or statute which the king establishes may be changed.'"

Consider This **The Plot Revealed**

Now, for the first time, the wicked design of the counselors flashed across Darius' mind! He saw that their motivation was not zeal for his kingly honor or glory, but jealousy against Daniel. By flattery, they had deceived him into signing the decree.

With remorse, Darius desperately sought for a way to deliver Daniel from his fate, but the constitutional lawyers of his day wove a seamless web. The decree was unchangeable.

Daniel 6:16–19 — Daniel in the Lions' Den

"So the king gave the command, and they brought Daniel and cast him into the den of lions. But the king spoke, saying to Daniel, 'Your God, whom you serve continually, He will deliver you.' Then a stone was brought and laid on the mouth of the den, and the king sealed it with his own signet ring and with the signets of his lords, that the purpose concerning Daniel might not be changed.

"Now the king went to his palace and spent the night fasting; and no musicians were brought before him. Also his sleep went from him. Then the king arose very early in the morning and went in haste to the den of lions."

Closer Look **A Remarkable Night**

A sorrowful and sympathetic king met Daniel at the lions' den. Darius had previously seen and heard enough to express faith in the ability of Daniel's God to deliver him.

God did not prevent Daniel's enemies from casting him into the lions' den. Instead, He permitted evil angels and wicked men to accomplish their purpose. Into the lions' den went a man greatly beloved by God—accompanied by his guardian angel, which no adverse power of demon, man or beast could touch. While the king spent a sleepless night in the palace, Daniel must have spent one of the most remarkable nights of his life visiting with his angel!

Daniel 6:20–24 — The Angel Shuts the Lions' Mouths

"And when he came to the den, he cried out with a lamenting voice to Daniel. The king spoke, saying to Daniel, 'Daniel, servant of the living God, has your God, whom you serve continually, been able to deliver you from the lions?'

"Then Daniel said to the king, 'O king, live forever! My God sent His angel and shut the lions' mouths, so that they have not hurt me, because I was found innocent before Him; and also, O king, I have done no wrong before you.'

"Now the king was exceedingly glad for him, and commanded that they should take Daniel up out of the den. So Daniel was taken up out of the den, and no injury whatever was found on him, because he believed in his God.

"And the king gave the command, and they brought those men who had accused Daniel, and they cast them into the den of lions — them, their children, and their wives; and the lions overpowered them, and broke all their bones in pieces before they ever came to the bottom of the den."

Faithfulness Rewarded

Unwavering in his allegiance to God, and unyielding in his witness before his enemies, Daniel stood as an example of a pure and holy life. His conduct made a great impression upon Darius. This carried over into the reign of Cyrus, influencing him in favor of the Jewish people. In an account written by the Jewish historian, Flavius Josephus, Daniel's accusers said the reason the lions didn't kill and eat him was because Darius had fed them just before Daniel was thrown into the den (Flavius Josephus, *Antiquities of the Jews*, Book 10, Chapter 11).

It was to prove their accusation false that Darius had Daniel's enemies thrown into the lions' den, "*and the lions overpowered them, and broke all their bones in pieces before they ever came to the bottom of the den.*"

Daniel 6:25–28 — Darius Magnifies God

Then King Darius wrote:

"*To all peoples, nations, and languages that dwell in all the earth:*
Peace be multiplied to you.
I make a decree that in every dominion of my kingdom men must tremble
and fear before the God of Daniel.
For He is the living God,
And steadfast forever;
His kingdom is the one which shall not be destroyed,

And His dominion shall endure to the end.

He delivers and rescues,

And He works signs and wonders

In heaven and on earth,

Who has delivered Daniel from the power of the lions.

"*So this Daniel prospered in the reign of Darius and in the reign of Cyrus the Persian.*"

Consider This The influence of Daniel, Ezra, Zerubbabel, Nehemiah, Mordecai, and Esther upon the kings and people of the Medo-Persian Empire was, and is, a testimony of their commitment to the Lord. In His love and mercy, God provided living examples to show this pagan nation the way of salvation.

The second section of the book of Daniel begins with the second chapter, and ends with the seventh chapter. Since this section is about what was happening in Babylon, it is written in the Aramaic language. It was after his lions' den experience that Daniel received the greater of prophecies concerning the latter days. The vision he received in the seventh chapter parallels the dream Nebuchadnezzar had in the second chapter, both of them beginning with the nation of Babylon, and ending with the Coming of Christ.

The prophecies of Daniel and Revelation are of utmost importance, since they explain events that are taking place at this very time in earth's history, and what will happen in the future.

DANIEL 7

1 In the first year of Belshazzar king of Babylon, Daniel had a dream and visions of his head while on his bed. Then he wrote down the dream, telling the main facts.

2 Daniel spoke, saying, "I saw in my vision by night, and behold, the four winds of heaven were stirring up the Great Sea.

3 And four great beasts came up from the sea, each different from the other.

4 The first was like a lion, and had eagle's wings. I watched till its wings were plucked off; and it was lifted up from the earth and made to stand on two feet like a man, and a man's heart was given to it.

5 "And suddenly another beast, a second, like a bear. It was raised up on one side, and had three ribs in its mouth between its teeth. And they said thus to it: 'Arise, devour much flesh!'

6 "After this I looked, and there was another, like a leopard, which had on its back four wings of a bird. The beast also had four heads, and dominion was given to it.

7 "After this I saw in the night visions, and behold, a fourth beast, dreadful and terrible, exceedingly strong. It had huge iron teeth; it was devouring, breaking in pieces, and trampling the residue with its feet. It was different from all the beasts that were before it, and it had ten horns.

8 I was considering the horns, and there was another horn, a little one, coming up among them, before whom three of the first horns were plucked out by the roots. And there, in this horn, were eyes like the eyes of a man, and a mouth speaking pompous words.

9 "I watched till thrones were put
    in place,
And the Ancient of Days was
    seated;
His garment was white as snow,
And the hair of His head was like
    pure wool.
His throne was a fiery flame,
Its wheels a burning fire;
10 A fiery stream issued
And came forth from before Him.
A thousand thousands ministered
    to Him;
Ten thousand times ten thousand
    stood before Him.
The court was seated,
And the books were opened.

11 "I watched then because of the sound of the pompous words which the horn was speaking; I watched till the beast was slain, and its body destroyed and given

to the burning flame.

12 As for the rest of the beasts, they had their dominion taken away, yet their lives were prolonged for a season and a time.

13 "I was watching in the night visions,

And behold, One like the Son of Man,

Coming with the clouds of heaven!

He came to the Ancient of Days,

And they brought Him near before Him.

14 Then to Him was given dominion and glory and a kingdom,

That all peoples, nations, and languages should serve Him.

His dominion is an everlasting dominion,

Which shall not pass away,

And His kingdom the one

Which shall not be destroyed.

15 "I, Daniel, was grieved in my spirit within my body, and the visions of my head troubled me. **16** I came near to one of those who stood by, and asked him the truth of all this. So he told me and made known to me the interpretation of these things:

17 'Those great beasts, which are four, are four kings which arise out of the earth. **18** But the saints of the Most High shall receive the kingdom, and possess the kingdom forever, even forever and ever.'

19 "Then I wished to know the truth about the fourth beast, which was different from all the others, exceedingly dreadful, with its teeth of iron and its nails of bronze, which devoured, broke in pieces, and trampled the residue with its feet;

20 and the ten horns that were on its head, and the other horn which came up, before which three fell, namely, that horn which had eyes and a mouth which spoke pompous words, whose appearance was greater than his fellows.

21 "I was watching; and the same horn was making war against the saints, and prevailing against them, **22** until the Ancient of Days came, and a judgment was made in favor of the saints of the Most High, and the time came for the saints to possess the kingdom.

23 "Thus he said:

'The fourth beast shall be

A fourth kingdom on earth,

Which shall be different from all other kingdoms,

And shall devour the whole earth,

Trample it and break it in pieces.

24 The ten horns are ten kings

Who shall arise from this kingdom.

And another shall rise after them;

He shall be different from the first ones,

And shall subdue three kings.

25 He shall speak pompous words against the Most High,

Shall persecute the saints of the Most High,
And shall intend to change times and law.
Then the saints shall be given into his hand
For a time and times and half a time.

26 'But the court shall be seated,
And they shall take away his dominion,
To consume and destroy it forever.
27 Then the kingdom and dominion,
And the greatness of the kingdoms under the whole heaven,
Shall be given to the people, the saints of the Most High.
His kingdom is an everlasting kingdom,
And all dominions shall serve and obey Him.'

28 "This is the end of the account. As for me, Daniel, my thoughts greatly troubled me, and my countenance changed; but I kept the matter in my heart."

CHAPTER 7

Four Great Beasts

Inside this Chapter

Daniel 7:1–8 — Four Great Beasts

"In the first year of Belshazzar king of Babylon, Daniel had a dream and visions of his head while on his bed. Then he wrote down the dream, telling the main facts.

"Daniel spoke, saying, 'I saw in my vision by night, and behold, the four winds of heaven were stirring up the Great Sea. And four great beasts came up from the sea, each different from the other. The first was like a lion, and had eagle's wings. I watched till its wings were plucked off; and it was lifted up from the earth and made to stand on two feet like a man, and a man's heart was given to it.

"'And suddenly another beast, a second, like a bear. It was raised up on one side, and had three ribs in its mouth between its teeth. And they said thus to it: "Arise, devour much flesh!"

"'After this I looked, and there was another, like a leopard, which had on its back four wings of a bird. The beast also had four heads, and dominion was given to it.

"'After this I saw in the night visions, and behold, a fourth beast, dreadful and terrible, exceedingly strong. It had huge iron teeth; it was devouring, breaking in pieces, and trampling the residue with its feet. It was different from all the beasts that were before it, and it had ten horns. I was considering the horns, and there was another horn, a little one, coming up among them, before whom three of the first horns were plucked out by the roots. And there, in this horn, were eyes like the eyes of a man, and a mouth speaking pompous words.'"

Daniel 7:1–2 — Prophetic Symbolism

"In the first year of Belshazzar king of Babylon, Daniel had a dream and visions of his head while on his bed. Then he wrote down the dream, telling the main facts.

"Daniel spoke, saying, 'I saw in my vision by night, and behold, the four winds of heaven were stirring up the Great Sea.'"

The visions of Daniel are not in chronological order. Yet they build one upon another, with subsequent visions often repeating, and expanding upon, previous ones. As a result, to be fully understood, each vision requires understanding of the previous ones. As we go through the prophetic visions, Scripture will open our understanding, so that by the end of the prophecy it will all fit together.

God uses water in Bible prophecy to represent people, nations, and tongues. *"And he said to me, 'The waters which you saw, where the harlot sits, are people, multitudes, nations, and tongues.'"* Revelation 17:15.

In Jeremiah 49:35–37, wind is used to symbolize war and strife. Revelation 7:1 also uses this symbolism: *"After these things I saw four angels standing at the four corners of the earth, holding the four winds of the earth, that the wind should not blow on the earth, or the sea, or on any tree."*

In this vision, Daniel saw the wind blowing on the water, which meant that there was war or strife among the nations.

Daniel 7:3 — Beasts in Bible Prophecy

"And four great beasts came up from the sea, each different from the other."

Beasts in Bible prophecy represent kingdoms/nations (7:23), just as the eagle symbolizes the United States of America, and the lion depicts England, etc.

As the angel Gabriel interpreted the vision for Daniel, he made clear what the beasts represented. *"Those great beasts, which are four, are four kings (kingdoms) which arise out of the earth."* Daniel 7:17.

Daniel 7:4 — Babylon as a Lion

"The first was like a lion, and had eagle's wings. I watched till its wings were plucked off; and it was lifted up from the earth and made to stand on two feet like a man, and a man's heart was given to it."

Jeremiah 4:7 depicts Babylon as a lion. Historically, the Lion represented Babylon— the richest and most powerful kingdom on earth. When archaeologists of the British Museum excavated the ruins of Babylon, they found statues of lions with eagle's wings—a common symbol representing the speed with which Babylon conquered. In a few years, Nebuchadnezzar had captured most of the then-known world.

Babylon overthrew Assyria in 605 B.C., and Nebuchadnezzar ruled for 40 of the 70 years the kingdom existed. "Plucked off" represents the fact that Babylon's period of conquest had come to an end.

Because of Nebuchadnezzar's conversion, the lion is pictured as having a man's heart. The lion corresponds to the head of gold in Daniel 2.

Closer Look | *Daniel 7:5 — Medo-Persia as the Bear*

"And suddenly another beast, a second, like a bear. It was raised up on one side, and had three ribs in its mouth between its teeth. And they said thus to it: 'Arise, devour much flesh!'"

Darius the Mede and Cyrus the Persian formed an alliance to overthrow Babylon. Pictured in Scripture as a slow and cumbersome bear, they made their attack on Babylon, overthrowing it in 539 B.C.

By describing the bear as being raised up on one side, the vision pictures the fact that Persia was the stronger of the two countries.

The three ribs in its mouth represented the nations overthrown by the bear (Medo-Persia). Those three ribs were Egypt in 535 B.C., Babylon in 539 B.C., and Lydia in 546 B.C..

Closer Look | *Daniel 7:6 — Greece as a Leopard*

"After this I looked, and there was another, like a leopard, which had on its back four wings of a bird. The beast also had four heads, and dominion was given to it."

The leopard, like the belly and thighs of bronze in the image of Daniel 2, depicts the kingdom of Greece. Alexander the Great vanquished Darius in the Battle of Arbela, in 331 B.C. The four wings represent the swiftness with which

Alexander conquered the world. By the age of 30, he had nothing left to conquer.

Alexander returned from his campaign suffering from malaria and drunkenness.

Aware that he was dying, he called for his four leading generals. They asked to whom he would bestow the empire, and he replied, "To the strongest."

After Alexander's death, his kingdom was eventually divided among his four leading generals, as follows: Cassander reigned over Macedonia and Greece, Lysimachus ruled Thrace and Bithynia, Ptolomy controlled Egypt, and Seleucus ruled Syria. This is why the leopard has four heads.

Closer Look — *Daniel 7:7 — Pagan Rome the Terrible Beast*

"After this I saw in the night visions, and behold, a fourth beast, dreadful and terrible, exceedingly strong. It had huge iron teeth; it was devouring, breaking in pieces, and trampling the residue with its feet. It was different from all the beasts that were before it, and it had ten horns."

The fourth beast with iron teeth is the same as the legs of iron in Daniel 2. The takeover of the Grecian Empire was gradual, but by 168 B.C., the Romans were very much in control. The great iron teeth portray the way in which Rome devoured both nations and peoples in its conquests.

As the Scripture describes, what Rome did not destroy, it brought into slavery, *"trampling the residue with its feet."* Daniel 7:7.

It was Rome's policy to subjugate its enemies permanently, until Roman laws, religion, language, and customs extended over the entire known world. Rome ruled until 476 A.D., the longest of any of these nations. At that time, the Germanic tribes began invading the Roman Empire, breaking it into pieces, and finally, into ten parts (ten horns).

The ten divisions of the Roman Empire are as follows: Alamanni, Ostrogoths, Visigoths, Franks, Vandals, Suevi, Burgundians, Heruli,

Anglo-Saxons, and Lombards. These Germanic tribes became the nations of Western Europe. The ten horns represent the same tribes as the toes of the image in Daniel 2. God gives more detail about this dreadful beast in the verses that follow.

Daniel 7:8 — The Little Horn

"I was considering the horns, and there was another horn, a little one, coming up among them, before whom three of the first horns were plucked out by the roots. And there, in this horn, were eyes like the eyes of a man, and a mouth speaking pompous words."

Daniel 7:8 lists four points that identify the Little Horn:

First Point: *Comes Up Among Them*

"Coming up among them."

One does not have to search the world over to find where the "Little Horn" is located. The Bible states that it would come up among the ten horns, which means that it had to arise out of Western Europe.

Second Point: *Plucked Out*

"Plucked out by the roots."

Of the ten tribes, the descendants of the Alamanni became the Germans; the Franks became the French; the Anglo-Saxons became the English, etc. However, there are no descendents of the Heruli, Vandals, or Ostrogoths. They were plucked out by the roots.

Why? The Heruli, Vandals, and Ostrogoths embraced a belief called Arianism, which taught that Christ was a created being, and therefore, not divine. The Papacy held to the Nicene Creed, which opposed this belief. During this point in history, Western Europe was in a transitional period, and the Christian Church was assuming civil power. Pagan Rome was becoming Papal Rome, and as a demonstration of her new civil power, Papal Rome destroyed (uprooted) all three tribes.

Third Point: *Eyes of a Man*

"Eyes like the eyes of a man."

This gives us an insight into the type of leadership that would direct the Little Horn —not by a council, parliament or senate, but by one man, whose word is law. The pope would become the voice of God for millions of people.

Fourth Point: *Speaking Pompous Words*

"A mouth speaking pompous words."

Many are the statements that fulfill this prophecy. Since we will explore this in greater detail later, only one statement is listed here:

"The pope is as it were God on earth, sole sovereign of the faithful of Christ, chief, king of kings, having plenitude of power" (Lucius Ferraris, *Prompia Bibliotheca*, Vol. VI, p. 29).

Daniel 7:9–10 — *Judgment Scene*

"I watched till thrones were put in place,

And the Ancient of Days was seated;

His garment was white as snow,

And the hair of His head was like pure wool.

His throne was a fiery flame,

Its wheels a burning fire;

A fiery stream issued

And came forth from before Him.

A thousand thousands ministered to Him;

Ten thousand times ten thousand stood before Him.

The court was seated,

And the books were opened."

Court in Session

According to verse 26, this time of judgment occurs when the Little Horn loses its power. *"But the court shall be seated, and they shall take away his dominion, to consume and destroy it forever."* Daniel 7:26.

Daniel saw different scenes of the closing events of the great controversy between Christ and Satan. This is why he repeated, *"I watched."* Daniel 7:9.

In vision, Daniel was taken from the actions of the Little Horn, to The Courtroom of Heaven. Here, the Ancient of Days sat in judgment, surrounded by an innumerable company of angels. This change of scenes, from earth to Heaven, takes place several times in this chapter.

Daniel 7:11–12 — Rise and Fall of Nations

"I watched then because of the sound of the pompous words which the horn was speaking; I watched till the beast was slain, and its body destroyed and given to the burning flame. As for the rest of the beasts, they had their dominion taken away, yet their lives were prolonged for a season and a time."

Beast Slain

Daniel saw the end of the system symbolized by the beast, which will be destroyed at the Second Coming of Christ. The other beasts represented nations that were overthrown, but allowed to live on. For example, it took years for Rome to do away with the influence of Greece. For this reason, verse 12 states, *"Yet their lives were prolonged for a season and a time."* Now the scene changes again to the judgment in Heaven.

Daniel 7:13–14 — The Son of Man

"I was watching in the night visions,
And behold, One like the Son of Man,
Coming with the clouds of heaven!
He came to the Ancient of Days,
And they brought Him near before Him.
Then to Him was given dominion and glory and a kingdom,
That all peoples, nations, and languages should serve Him.
His dominion is an everlasting dominion,
Which shall not pass away,
And His kingdom the one
Which shall not be destroyed."

Consider This **Christ the Mediator**

To get the real significance of this text, read verses 9, 10, 13, and 14. They give a more complete picture of what Daniel saw in Heaven.

This passage is not referring to the Second Coming of Christ to this earth, but to the *"Ancient of Days."* God revealed to Daniel the order of events that are to take place during a period known as the *"time of the end."* This is emphasized as we go through the chapter.

The vision depicts Christ coming before His Father, the *"Ancient of Days,"* during the judgment taking place in Heaven. If we face the judgment alone, we each know in our inmost souls that we are guilty, *"For all have sinned and fall short of the glory of God."* Romans 3:23. Jesus, as the "Son of Man," is our only hope. Hallelujah! He has redeemed us from the condemnation of the law, and goes before His Father as Mediator for those who have accepted Him as their Savior. When His intercession is completed, He will come back to set up His Everlasting Kingdom.

Daniel 7:15–16 — Daniel Troubled

"I, Daniel, was grieved in my spirit within my body, and the visions of my head troubled me. I came near to one of those who stood by, and asked him the truth of all this. So he told me and made known to me the interpretation of these things."

Consider This **Angel to Explain**

Daniel was distressed because he did not understand what he was being shown, until the angel explained it to him. It is imperative that we understand these verses, for they cover the period from Daniel's day to the end of time.

Daniel 7:17–22 — The Interpretation

"'Those great beasts, which are four, are four kings which arise out of the earth. But the saints of the Most High shall receive the kingdom, and possess the kingdom forever, even forever and ever.'

"Then I wished to know the truth about the fourth beast, which was different from all the others, exceedingly dreadful, with its teeth of iron and its nails of bronze, which devoured, broke in pieces, and trampled the

residue with its feet; and the ten horns that were on its head, and the other horn which came up, before which three fell, namely, that horn which had eyes and a mouth which spoke pompous words, whose appearance was greater than his fellows.

"I was watching; and the same horn was making war against the saints, and prevailing against them, until the Ancient of Days came, and a judgment was made in favor of the saints of the Most High, and the time came for the saints to possess the kingdom."

Concern About the Fourth Beast

As the angel was explaining the vision, Daniel interrupted him and said, *"Tell me about the fourth beast."* This beast was of great interest to Daniel, because it was *"making war against the saints, and prevailing against them."*

To relieve Daniel's anxiety regarding the saints, the angel assured him that *"judgment was made in favor of the saints."* By reading verses 13 and 22 together, the judgment scene is complete. It reads as follows: *"I was watching in the night visions, and behold, One like the Son of Man, coming with the clouds of heaven! He came to the Ancient of Days, and they brought Him near before Him…. And a judgment was made in favor of the saints of the Most High, and the time came for the saints to possess the kingdom."*

Thank God for the ministry of Jesus Christ in our behalf!

Daniel 7:23–25 — Little Horn Identified

"Thus he said:
'The fourth beast shall be
A fourth kingdom on earth,
Which shall be different from all other kingdoms,
And shall devour the whole earth,
Trample it and break it in pieces.
The ten horns are ten kings
Who shall arise from this kingdom.
And another shall rise after them;
He shall be different from the first ones,

And shall subdue three kings.

He shall speak pompous words against the Most High,

Shall persecute the saints of the Most High,

And shall intend to change times and law.

Then the saints shall be given into his hand

For a time and times and half a time.'"

Pagan and Papal Rome

After reassuring Daniel about the saints, the angel Gabriel continued to explain the fourth beast, which is the kingdom of Pagan Rome (as we discovered in verse 7.) On the head of this beast are ten horns, representing ten kingdoms that would arise as the Germanic tribes became the nations of Western Europe (see Daniel 7:7 and 2:41–43).

God spends more time in Scripture explaining the Little Horn power than any other power. The Bible lists nine identifying points of the Little Horn power, so that there can be no question as to its identity:

First Point: *Comes Up Among Them*

"Coming up among them" Daniel 7:8.

The ten horns were ten Germanic tribes called Goths, or Barbarians, which conquered Pagan Rome. They became the nations of Western Europe, fulfilling Daniel 7:24, which states they would "arise from this kingdom" (Pagan Rome).

Daniel 7:8 pictures the Little Horn as *"coming up among"* the ten horns. These Germanic tribes began to overthrow the Roman Empire in 476 A.D., and Papal Rome is the only power that fits into this place (Western Europe) and time (after 476 A.D.).

Second Point: *Shall Rise After Them*

"Another shall rise after them" Daniel 7:24.

The Little Horn power had to come on the scene of action after 476 A.D., and history records that Papal Rome came into power in 538 A.D. The fourth point will explain this in detail.

Third Point: *Different From the First Ones*

"He shall be different from the first ones" Daniel 7:24.

Horns represent kingdoms. As with the ten horns among which it grew, the Little Horn is not a single individual, as is commonly thought, and taught. In addition, this horn is different. The ten Germanic tribes were pagan and political powers; but Papal Rome is a combination of both church <u>and</u> state, of both religious <u>and</u> political powers. In 538 A.D., Papal Rome began to gain civil power, and that civil power enabled her to 'enforce' her laws and dogmas.

Fourth Point: *Subdue Three Kings*

"Shall subdue three kings" Daniel 7:24.

Justinian was the Emperor of Rome at this time. He saw his empire being taken away by the Goths, who had overrun the kingdom.

Three tribes, the Heruli, Vandals, and Ostrogoths had accepted a belief called Arianism, which taught that Jesus Christ was a created being, and therefore, not divine. The Catholic Church opposed this belief.

Since Justinian had resolved to purge the church of that heresy, he joined forces with the Catholic Church to destroy these three tribes, and "three of the first horns were plucked out by the roots." Daniel 7:8.

Today, descendants exist of all the Germanic tribes except the Heruli, Vandals, and Ostrogoths. Through the joint efforts of the Catholic Church and Pagan Rome, they were completely eradicated. The last to be annihilated were the Ostrogoths, in 538 A.D. With this victory, history states that the Pope seized the scepter, and stepped into the seat of Caesar. This began the reign of Papal Rome.

Fifth Point: *Eyes of a Man*

"Eyes like the eyes of a man" Daniel 7:8.

Eyes are symbolic of intelligence. The barbarians were generally illiterate. In contrast, the cunning foresight, subtlety, and secret diplomacy of the Papacy—and especially the Jesuits—are a well-known fact.

The Scripture sometimes pictures horns as having *"crowns"* (Revelation 13:1), meaning that a monarch rules these powers or nations, rather than a council, parliament, or senate. The Pope is the visible head of the

Papacy, and his authority is not to be questioned. The *"eyes like the eyes of a man"* Daniel 7:8 refers to the leadership of these men.

Sixth Point: *Speak Pompous Words*

"Speak pompous words against the Most High" Daniel 7:25.

This is the power that Paul speaks of in 2 Thessalonians 2:4, *"... He sits as God in the temple of God, showing himself that he is God."*

The following statements confirm this fact:

"The pope is of so great dignity and so exalted that he is not a mere man, but as it were God, and the vicar of God." (Lucius Ferraris, *Prompia Bibliotheca* Vol. VI, p. 26.)

"We [the popes] hold upon this earth the place of God Almighty." (The Great Encyclical Letter of Pope Leo the XIII (New York, NY: Benziger Brothers, 1903) p. 304.)

"For thou the popes art the shepherd, thou art the physician, thou art the director, thou art the husbandman, finally, thou art another God on earth." (Christopher Marcellus, *Oration in the Fifth Lateran Council,* Session IV, Vol. 32, col. 761.)

Seventh Point: *Persecute the Saints*

"Shall persecute the saints of the Most High" Daniel 7:25.

Historians tell us that the Papal Power is responsible for the death of millions of people. For example, the following history books detail the persecution known as the Spanish Inquisition, the persecution of the Waldensian people and the Dutch, and the Saint Bartholomew's Day Massacre:

- *The History of the Reformation* of the 16th Century, by Jean-Henri Merle d'Aubigné
- *The Great Controversy*, by Ellen G. White
- *Foxe's Book of Martyrs*, by John Foxe
- *Stories of the Reformation in England and Scotland*, by Ruth Gordon Short
- *Here I Stand: A Life of Martin Luther*, by Roland H. Bainton

It is common knowledge that on May 24, 1995, Pope John Paul II issued a world apology for the persecuting role taken by the Catholic Church during the period that followed the Protestant Reformation.

Eighth Point: *Change Times and Laws*

"Intend to change times and laws" Daniel 7:25.

God is the One who predetermines the events of life. *"To everything there is a season, a time for every purpose under heaven."* Ecclesiastes 3:1.

Concerning the changing of times, the Little Horn attempted to change the course of history by exercising the prerogative of God to set up kings, and to take them down.

The power that makes laws, and changes them, is the one which is in control. This is why the Scripture states, *"There is one Lawgiver, who is able to save and to destroy."* James 4:12.

The Papacy claims to have this prerogative, which belongs only to God: "The pope can modify divine law, since his power is not of man, but of God, and he acts in the place of God upon earth, with the fullest power of binding and loosing his sheep." (Lucius Ferraris, *Prompia Bibliotheca*, Vol. VIII, art. Papa, II.)

Comparing the Ten Commandments in a Catholic Catechism with Scripture reflects the fact that the papacy has exercised that prerogative. The second commandment in Exodus 20:4–6, which states, *"You shall not make for yourself a carved image—any likeness of anything that is in heaven above, or that is in the earth beneath, or that is in the water under the earth; you shall not bow down to them nor serve them ...,"* has been removed. God's third commandment became her second, and His fourth commandment became her third. In order to still have "Ten" Commandments, she then divided God's tenth commandment into two, making it numbers nine *and* ten. In addition, she changed God's fourth commandment from ninety-four words, to eight!

The fourth commandment is an example of changing both *"times and laws."*) The seventh day Sabbath, which God blessed, hallowed, and sanctified (see Genesis 2:1–3 and Exodus 20:8–11,) was done away with by the Catholic Church. They replaced God's seventh day Bible Sabbath with Sunday, the first day of the week, a day whose very name was given to it by pagan worshipers of the sun.

The Papacy even admits that this so-called "change" (for God alone can *truly* change His Law) was its accomplishment, and that there is no Scriptural authority for this change. Instead, the Papacy claims to have made this change due to a sense of its own authority in religious matters; and it ridicules those Protestant denominations that worship on Sunday just as the Catholics do, yet claim to follow the Bible alone as the rule of faith.

"The church, after changing the day of rest from the Jewish Sabbath of the seventh day of the week to the first made the Third Commandment refer to Sunday as the day to be kept holy as the Lord's Day." (*The Catholic Encyclopedia* Vol. 4, p. 153) To read which day is truly the Lord's day, see Isaiah 58:13–14.

Ninth Point: *Time, Times and Half a Time*

"Time and times and half a time" Daniel 7:25.

God has given a rule that, in Bible prophecy, a day represents one literal year (see Ezekiel 4:6 and Numbers 14:34). In Scripture, the term "time" represents one year (Daniel 4:25). Using God's day-for-a-year principle, *"times"* represents two years, and half a time represents half a year.

There are 360 days in a biblical year, and the Bible's narrative of the great flood holds a key to this time-reckoning principle.

Genesis 7:11 tells us that the flood began in the *"… second month, the seventeenth day of the month."* Genesis 8:4 states that the waters abated, and the ark rested on Mt. Ararat, on the *"… seventh month, the seventeenth day of the month."* In other words, the floodwaters covered the earth for five months.

Genesis 7:24 and 8:3 speak of that period of time as the *"hundred and fifty days."*

Therefore, since five Biblical months equal 150 days, one month equals 30 days (150 ÷ 5 = 30). One Biblical year of twelve months equals 360 days; two years equals 720 days; and half a year equals 180 days; totaling 1,260 days. Each prophetic day represents one literal year, so we arrive at 1,260 years in which the Little Horn was to be in power.

The Papacy came into power in 538 A.D. When we add 1,260 years to 538 A.D., we arrive at 1798 A.D. History refers to this time period as the period of Papal Supremacy.

In 1798 A.D., Napoleon's general, Alexandre Berthier, marched into Rome and ended the Papal power. The 1941 edition of *The Encyclopedia Americana* records the event: "In 1798, he (Berthier, Napoleon's general) ... made his entrance into Rome, abolished the papal government, and established a secular one."

Daniel 7:26–27 — Judgment to Begin

"'But the court shall be seated,
And they shall take away his dominion,
To consume and destroy it forever.
Then the kingdom and dominion,
And the greatness of the kingdoms under the whole heaven,
Shall be given to the people, the saints of the Most High.
His kingdom is an everlasting kingdom,
And all dominions shall serve and obey Him.'"

Four Kingdoms and the Second Coming

The period covered by the book of Daniel encompasses Daniel's day, to the Second Coming of Christ. Please note that the second and seventh chapters explain four kingdoms: Babylon, Medo-Persia, Greece, and Rome. The seventh chapter expands upon the definition of the fourth kingdom.

Daniel explains the transformation of Rome—from Pagan Rome to Papal Rome—and gives its history in just a few sentences. *"Behold, a fourth beast, dreadful and terrible, exceedingly strong. It had huge iron teeth; it was devouring, breaking in pieces, and trampling the residue with its feet. It was different from all the beasts that were before it, and it had ten horns. I was considering the horns, and there was another horn, a little one, coming up among them, before whom three of the first horns were plucked out by the roots. And there, in this horn, were eyes like the eyes of a man, and a mouth speaking pompous words."* Daniel 7:7–8.

The entire book of Daniel is dedicated to the discussion of these four beasts/kingdoms.

The book of Revelation follows this same format, and if that concept is clear to you, it will make prophecy much easier to understand. Daniel goes into great detail to ensure we understand that Rome (the fourth kingdom) will continue until the Second Coming of the Lord.

Key to Prophecy **Last Day Events**
The seventh chapter contains the sequence of three, critical, last day events. God considers these events so vital that He repeats them three times:

Little Horn	Judgement Begins	Christ's Kingdom
Daniel 7:8 *And there was another horn, a little one, coming up among them*	**Daniel 7:9** *I watched till thrones were put in place, and the Ancient of Days was seated*	**Daniel 7:14** *Then to Him was given dominion and glory and a kingdom*
Daniel 7:21 *I was watching; and the same horn was making war against the saints*	**Daniel 7:22** *Until the Ancient of Days came, and a judgment was made in favor of the saints of the Most High*	**Daniel 7:22** *And the time came for the saints to possess the kingdom*
Daniel 7:24 *And another shall rise after them; He shall be different from the first ones*	**Daniel 7:26** *But the court shall be seated*	**Daniel 7:27** *His kingdom is an everlasting kingdom, And all dominions shall serve and obey Him*

The first event is the rise and fall of the Little Horn power. The next event to occur is the Judgment, and chapters 8 and 9 deal with that subject in detail. After the Judgment, Christ will set up His kingdom.

Consider This **Daniel 7:28 — Daniel Still Troubled**
"This is the end of the account. As for me, Daniel, my thoughts greatly troubled me, and my countenance changed; but I kept the matter in my heart."

Kept the Matter in His Heart

In answer to Daniel's questions, the angel Gabriel revealed the rise and fall of nations in amazing detail. He also disclosed how the followers of Christ will fare in the conflict—the great conflict between Christ and Satan.

It is imperative that we know the answers to these questions, for they apply to each one of us today.

DANIEL
PURE AND SIMPLE

CHAPTERS
8–12

Prophetic Section:
Original Language Hebrew

In Daniel chapters 8 and 11, the prophecies begin with Persia and end with the destruction of the Little Horn, or the king of the North, both being the same power. Written in the Hebrew language, these chapters explain what is to happen to God's people.

DANIEL 8

1 In the third year of the reign of King Belshazzar a vision appeared to me—to me, Daniel—after the one that appeared to me the first time.

2 I saw in the vision, and it so happened while I was looking, that I was in Shushan, the citadel, which is in the province of Elam; and I saw in the vision that I was by the River Ulai.

3 Then I lifted my eyes and saw, and there, standing beside the river, was a ram which had two horns, and the two horns were high; but one was higher than the other, and the higher one came up last.

4 I saw the ram pushing westward, northward, and southward, so that no animal could withstand him; nor was there any that could deliver from his hand, but he did according to his will and became great.

5 And as I was considering, suddenly a male goat came from the west, across the surface of the whole earth, without touching the ground; and the goat had a notable horn between his eyes.

6 Then he came to the ram that had two horns, which I had seen standing beside the river, and ran at him with furious power.

7 And I saw him confronting the ram; he was moved with rage against him, attacked the ram, and broke his two horns. There was no power in the ram to withstand him, but he cast him down to the ground and trampled him; and there was no one that could deliver the ram from his hand.

8 Therefore the male goat grew very great; but when he became strong, the large horn was broken, and in place of it four notable ones came up toward the four winds of heaven.

9 And out of one of them came a little horn which grew exceedingly great toward the south, toward the east, and toward the Glorious Land.

10 And it grew up to the host of heaven; and it cast down some of the host and some of the stars to the ground, and trampled them.

11 He even exalted himself as high as the Prince of the host; and by him the daily sacrifices were taken away, and the place of His sanctuary was cast down.

12 Because of transgression, an army was given over to the horn to oppose the daily sacrifices; and he cast truth down to the ground. He did all this and prospered.

13 Then I heard a holy one speaking; and another holy one said to that certain one who was speaking, "How long will the vision be, concerning the daily sacrifices and the transgression of desolation, the giving of both the sanctuary and the host to be trampled underfoot?"

14 And he said to me, "For two thousand three hundred days; then the sanctuary shall be cleansed."

15 Then it happened, when I, Daniel, had seen the vision and was seeking the meaning, that suddenly there stood before me one having the appearance of a man.

16 And I heard a man's voice between the banks of the Ulai, who called, and said, "Gabriel, make this man understand the vision."

17 So he came near where I stood, and when he came I was afraid and fell on my face; but he said to me, "Understand, son of man, that the vision refers to the time of the end."

18 Now, as he was speaking with me, I was in a deep sleep with my face to the ground; but he touched me, and stood me upright.

19 And he said, "Look, I am making known to you what shall happen in the latter time of the indignation; for at the appointed time the end shall be.

20 The ram which you saw, having the two horns — they are the kings of Media and Persia.

21 And the male goat is the kingdom of Greece. The large horn that is between its eyes is the first king.

22 As for the broken horn and the four that stood up in its place, four kingdoms shall arise out of that nation, but not with its power.

23 "And in the latter time of their kingdom,
When the transgressors have reached their fullness,
A king shall arise,
Having fierce features,
Who understands sinister schemes.

24 His power shall be mighty, but not by his own power;
He shall destroy fearfully,
And shall prosper and thrive;
He shall destroy the mighty, and also the holy people.

25 "Through his cunning
He shall cause deceit to prosper under his rule;
And he shall exalt himself in his heart.
He shall destroy many in their prosperity.
He shall even rise against the Prince of princes;
But he shall be broken without human means.

26 "And the vision of the evenings and mornings
Which was told is true;
Therefore seal up the vision,
For it refers to many days in the future."

27 And I, Daniel, fainted and was sick for days; afterward I arose and went about the king's business. I was astonished by the vision, but no one understood it.

CHAPTER 8

The Ram and the Goat

Inside this Chapter

Daniel 8:1–2 — Introduction to Chapter 8

"In the third year of the reign of King Belshazzar a vision appeared to me— to me, Daniel—after the one that appeared to me the first time. I saw in the vision, and it so happened while I was looking, that I was in Shushan, the citadel, which is in the province of Elam; and I saw in the vision that I was by the River Ulai."

Closer Look | **Second Vision**

When we reached the end of chapter seven, Daniel was troubled. While in vision two years later, he saw himself in Shushan (known today as Susa), the capital of Persia, in the province of Elam, by the river Ulai (known today as Kerkhah). Tradition tells us that Daniel was buried in this area.

Daniel 8:3–4 — Vision of the Ram

"Then I lifted my eyes and saw, and there, standing beside the river, was a ram which had two horns, and the two horns were high; but one was higher than the other, and the higher one came up last. I saw the ram pushing westward, northward, and southward, so that no animal could withstand him; nor was there any that could deliver from his hand, but he did according to his will and became great."

Key to Prophecy | **Medo-Persia, the Ram**

Babylon was in its last days, about to be overthrown by Cyrus, the Persian. As a result, this prophecy excludes Babylon and begins with the kingdom that succeeded it, portrayed by a ram with two horns. In verse 20, Daniel identifies Medo-Persia by name, and this ties in perfectly with what we learned in chapters 2 and 7.

Both the arms and breast of silver, and the bear with three ribs in its mouth, represent Medo-Persia. This is the third time that Scripture identifies Medo-Persia as the kingdom following Babylon. These verses confirm that God uses beasts to represent governments or nations.

The two horns portray the union of the Persian and Median powers, which formed Medo-Persia, and one horn being higher than the other indicates the superior strength of Persia. As Scripture states, Persia joined the federation last.

The ram pushed "westward, northward, and southward." No nation was able to stop it.

Medo-Persia extended its borders all the way from India to Ethiopia.

The countries of Egypt, Lydia, and Babylon all succumbed to the butting of the ram.

Daniel 8:5–7 — Vision of the Goat

"And as I was considering, suddenly a male goat came from the west, across the surface of the whole earth, without touching the ground; and the goat had a notable horn between his eyes. Then he came to the ram that had two horns, which I had seen standing beside the river, and ran at him with furious power. And I saw him confronting the ram; he was moved with rage against him, attacked the ram, and broke his two horns. There was no power in the ram to withstand him, but he cast him down to the ground and trampled him; and there was no one that could deliver the ram from his hand."

Greece the Goat

The speed with which the goat moved across the earth rightly depicts how quickly the Grecian empire conquered, under the leadership of Alexander the Great. Just as verse 20 tells us what the ram represents, verse 21 tells us exactly what the goat represents— Greece—the same kingdom as the belly and thighs of bronze of the image in Daniel 2, and the leopard in Daniel 7. Once more, for the third time, the Scripture confirms the succession of the kingdoms, for Greece would follow Medo-Persia.

In 331 B.C., on the plains of Arbela, Alexander, with 40,000 men, faced Darius III Codomannus, whose army numbered one million. Instituting a new type of warfare, Alexander overthrew him and became master of the then-known world.

Daniel 8:8 — The Notable Horn

"Therefore the male goat grew very great; but when he became strong, the large horn was broken, and in place of it four notable ones came up toward the four winds of heaven."

Key to Prophecy *Broken and Divided*

After marching his men for seven years without going home, Alexander and his soldiers returned home from India, undefeated. He was just 32 years of age, and had conquered everything in his path. At the height of his strength and power, while celebrating his victories in the city of Babylon, Alexander succumbed to drunkenness and malaria.

Summoning his four leading generals before he died, Alexander told them that he was leaving his empire "To the strongest!"

At this time, the phrase "Toward the four winds of heaven" was played-out in history. Each of Alexander's four leading generals received a portion of the Grecian Empire: Seleucus became the ruler of Syria in the east; Lysimachus ruled over Asia Minor to the north; Cassander ruled over Macedonia in the west; and Ptolomy ruled over Egypt to the south.

Located between Syria and Egypt was the land of Palestine, over which many wars were fought.

Daniel 8:9–12 — The Little Horn

"And out of one of them came a little horn which grew exceedingly great toward the south, toward the east, and toward the Glorious Land. And it grew up to the host of heaven; and it cast down some of the host and some of the stars to the ground, and trampled them. He even exalted himself as high as the Prince of the host; and by him the daily sacrifices were taken away, and the place of His sanctuary was cast down. Because of transgression, an army was given over to the horn to oppose the daily sacrifices; and he cast truth down to the ground. He did all this and prospered."

Key to Prophecy ***Horn Against the Daily – Points to Consider***
First Point: *Birth of the Roman Empire*

The statement in verse 9, *"Out of one of them came a little horn,"* describes the fact that the Little Horn power would arise from within one of the four divisions of Alexander's empire, those described in verse 8. Since the Little Horn power pushed to the south, east, and north, meaning it had to come from the west.

Of the four leading generals, Cassander proved to be the strongest. His kingdom grew to become the mighty Roman Empire, the *"Little Horn, which grew exceeding great"* (Daniel 8:9).

In fulfillment of verse 9, history records that Cassander's kingdom of Macedonia pushed *"toward the south;"* Egypt (which fell to Rome in 30 B.C.) pushed *"toward the east;"* and Syria (which fell to Rome in 65 B.C.) pushed north *"towards the Glorious Land;"* representing Palestine (which fell to Rome in 63 B.C.).

Second Point: *Antiochus Epiphanes*

In chapters 2, 7, 8, and 11 of Daniel, all the empires appear in identical order; the same order in which they appeared in history:

1. Babylon
2. Medo-Persia
3. Greece
4. Pagan Rome
5. The Divided Kingdoms
6. Papal Rome

Deviating from this order causes the prophecies to lose harmony, and creates great confusion.

Some people attempt to interject Antiochus Epiphanes as the Little Horn power, making it impossible to understand what the prophecies represent. Antiochus Epiphanes was one in a series of Seleucid kings. The beasts represented in these prophecies symbolize world powers, not individuals.

This same *"Little Horn"* is addressed in Daniel 7:21, 22 and 26, and it continues until the glorious Second Coming of Jesus. King Antiochus Epiphanes had been dead for approximately 164 years before the First Coming of Christ. Furthermore, most people today are familiar with the Grecian and Persian Empires, but very few know of Antiochus Epiphanes. Since the Little Horn power (Papal Rome) is greater than all of the preceding powers, it follows that it must be well-known in history, and widely-known in the world.

Third Point: *Jesus in Daniel*

"He even exalted himself as high as the Prince of the host" Daniel 8:11.

Daniel identifies *"the Prince of the host"* as Christ. In Daniel 8:25, a similar phrase is used, *"Prince of princes."* Jesus is referred to as *"Messiah the Prince*" in Daniel 9:25. Daniel 11:25, calls Him the *"Prince of the covenant."* All of these terms refer to Jesus, who was condemned, and crucified, under the authority of Pagan Rome.

Fourth Point: *The Daily Sacrifices*

"And by him [the Little Horn] the daily sacrifices were taken away" Daniel 8:11.

In this phrase, it is not the sacrifices that were being taken away, but the *"daily."* The word "sacrifices" does not appear in the original Hebrew text; it was added later to help clarify the meaning.

The Hebrew word for "daily" is "tamid," which means something that occurs on a regular basis. The offering of a sacrifice took place regularly each day: *"To stand every morning to thank and praise the Lord, and likewise at evening; and at every presentation of a burnt offering to the Lord on the Sabbaths and on the New Moons and on the set feasts, by number according to the ordinance governing them, regularly [tamid] before the Lord."* 1 Chronicles 23:30–31 (emphasis added).

The Hebrew word "tamid" is used for all the recurring worship services in the Old Testament, whether they came daily, weekly, monthly, or yearly.

Its meaning covered much more than the daily burnt offering in the temple, it encompassed everything involved with their daily worship of God. In short, the Little Horn was trying to take away their worship of God.

Daniel 12:11, ties the taking away of the "daily" with the *"abomination of desolation."* Christ spoke of this in Matthew 24:15, *"'Therefore when you see the "abomination of desolation," spoken of by Daniel the prophet, standing in the holy place' (whoever reads, let him understand)....."* This shows clearly that this event was to take place in the future.

In 70 A.D., Rome invaded the city of Jerusalem. Rome pitched banners in honor of its pagan gods on the holy grounds of the temple, eventually setting it on fire, and burning it to the ground. This resulted in the *"abomination of desolation,"* and an end to Israel's daily worship of God in the temple. This action established Rome as the Little Horn of Daniel 8. This scenario unfolds further as Daniel expands on what the future holds.

Daniel 8:13–14 — The Length of the Vision

"Then I heard a holy one speaking; and another holy one said to that certain one who was speaking, 'How long will the vision be, concerning the daily sacrifices and the transgression of desolation, the giving of both the sanctuary and the host to be trampled underfoot?'

"And he said to me, 'For two thousand three hundred days; then the sanctuary shall be cleansed.'"

Consider This

2,300 Days

Inspiration stresses an order of events three times in the seventh chapter of Daniel. The Little Horn of Daniel 7, (the Papal power) would go into captivity in 1798, after which the Judgment would begin. Once it is completed, God will set up His kingdom (Daniel 7:8–9, 14, 21–22, 27–28).

At the end of the seventh chapter, Daniel was troubled about the order and meaning of the events, so the angel Gabriel returned to clarify the vision. Gabriel explained that the Little Horn (Rome) would destroy the temple in Jerusalem and take away the daily sacrifice (Daniel 8:13), making the sanctuary (temple) desolate.

As Daniel listened to the conversation between the two holy ones, he heard a holy one ask how long this would continue, and Daniel was told, *"For two thousand three hundred days; then the sanctuary shall be cleansed."* Daniel 8:14.

We must remember that punctuation, including chapter breaks and numbers, did not exist at the time the book of Daniel was written. The explanation of Gabriel's answer does not come until chapter 9. The remainder of chapter 8 gives needed clarification. In fact, all the remaining chapters of Daniel are an explanation of the seventh chapter.

Daniel 8:15–19 — The Time of the End

"Then it happened, when I, Daniel, had seen the vision and was seeking the meaning, that suddenly there stood before me one having the appearance of a man. And I heard a man's voice between the banks of the Ulai, who called, and said, 'Gabriel, make this man understand the vision.' So he came near where I stood, and when he came I was afraid and fell on my face; but he said to me, 'Understand, son of man, that the vision refers to the time of the end.'

"Now, as he was speaking with me, I was in a deep sleep with my face to the ground; but he touched me, and stood me upright. And he said, 'Look, I am making known to you what shall happen in the latter time of the indignation; for at the appointed time the end shall be.'"

At the Appointed Time the End Shall Be

The angel Gabriel wants to make sure Daniel understands that the vision concerns the *"time of the end."* This phrase is used in chapters 8, 11, and 12, to depict the period of time from 1798 A.D., to the Second Coming of Christ.

The 1,260-year prophecy of Daniel 7:25, and Daniel 12:7, proves that the *"time of the end"* began in 1798 A.D. That is why the last chapters of Daniel are important to people living today. We are living in the "latter time," which is the *"time of the end."* Nevertheless, God always has a plan, an order in which events are to take place. They move like clockwork, *"for at the appointed time the end shall be."*

Daniel 8:20–22 — Interpretation of the Ram and the Goat

"The ram which you saw, having the two horns—they are the kings of Media and Persia. And the male goat is the kingdom of Greece. The large horn that is between its eyes is the first king. As for the broken horn and the four that stood up in its place, four kingdoms shall arise out of that nation, but not with its power."

It Can't Be Any Clearer

The angel repeated the vision, placing the kingdoms in order so that Daniel would understand. The ram was the coalition of Media and Persia. The male goat represented Greece. It was under the leadership of Alexander the Great, the *"large horn,"* that Greece rose to its greatest height. Greece's phase under Alexander's leadership was the first phase of the goat, and it ended with Alexander's death. Although Alexander's kingdom was in a chaotic state for a while, it eventually split into four divisions. Those four horns that came up in place of the first horn represented the final phase of the goat's power. Alexander's four leading generals succeeded in dividing his kingdom into four parts; however, none of them had the strength of Alexander's kingdom.

Daniel 8:23–25 — The Little Horn Revealed

"And in the latter time of their kingdom,
When the transgressors have reached their fullness,
A king shall arise,
Having fierce features,
Who understands sinister schemes.
His power shall be mighty, but not by his own power;
He shall destroy fearfully,
And shall prosper and thrive;
He shall destroy the mighty, and also the holy people.
Through his cunning
He shall cause deceit to prosper under his rule;
And he shall exalt himself in his heart.
He shall destroy many in their prosperity.
He shall even rise against the Prince of princes;
But he shall be broken without human means."

Consider This

Both Phases of Rome

As the Grecian Empire slowly faded away, Pagan Rome attained supremacy: *"A king shall arise, having fierce features, who understands sinister schemes."* Daniel 8:23. This description coincides with the picture of the fourth beast of Daniel 7, which represents Pagan Rome, and with the picture of the Little Horn—the Papacy. The angel's interpretation agrees with what was revealed in Daniel 2 and 7. When we apply it to Rome, as mentioned in the remarks on verse 9, it becomes clear.

Since Papal Rome was, in many respects, a continuation of the Roman Empire, there is a mingling of applications. Some points apply to both, while others apply to only one.

The authority of the Roman Empire was utilized by both Pagan and Papal Rome—such as in the crucifixion of Christ, and in the persecution of the Jewish, and Christian, peoples.

Both Pagan and Papal Rome did "destroy the mighty, and also the holy people." Daniel 8:24.

Papal Rome assumed the power and authority of Pagan Rome and became mighty, but as the text states, *"... not by his own power."* Daniel 8:24.

Yet, Scripture reveals that the power of Papal Rome will continue until the Second Coming of Christ, when it will *"be broken without human means."* Daniel 8:25.

Daniel 8:26–27 — Daniel's Sickness

"And the vision of the evenings and mornings

Which was told is true;

Therefore seal up the vision,

For it refers to many days in the future.'

And I, Daniel, fainted and was sick for days; afterward I arose and went about the king's business. I was astonished by the vision, but no one understood it."

Many Days in the Future

Gabriel had not yet begun to explain the 2,300 days mentioned in Daniel 8:14, which he said, *"is true"* in verse 26.

By this time, Daniel had received all he could bear. Therefore, the angel said, *"Seal up the vision."* Daniel 8:26. More would be revealed when Daniel was feeling better, and stronger. He not only needed to be about the king's business, he also needed time to pray for understanding of the vision.

DANIEL 9

1 In the first year of Darius the son of Ahasuerus, of the lineage of the Medes, who was made king over the realm of the Chaldeans—
2 in the first year of his reign I, Daniel, understood by the books the number of the years specified by the word of the Lord through Jeremiah the prophet, that He would accomplish seventy years in the desolations of Jerusalem.
3 Then I set my face toward the Lord God to make request by prayer and supplications, with fasting, sackcloth, and ashes.
4 And I prayed to the Lord my God, and made confession, and said, "O Lord, great and awesome God, who keeps His covenant and mercy with those who love Him, and with those who keep His commandments,
5 we have sinned and committed iniquity, we have done wickedly and rebelled, even by departing from Your precepts and Your judgments.
6 Neither have we heeded Your servants the prophets, who spoke in Your name to our kings and our princes, to our fathers and all the people of the land.
7 O Lord, righteousness belongs to You, but to us shame of face, as it is this day—to the men of Judah, to the inhabitants of Jerusalem and all Israel, those near and those far off in all the countries to which You have driven them, because of the unfaithfulness which they have committed against You.
8 "O Lord, to us belongs shame of face, to our kings, our princes, and our fathers, because we have sinned against You.
9 To the Lord our God belong mercy and forgiveness, though we have rebelled against Him.
10 We have not obeyed the voice of the Lord our God, to walk in His laws, which He set before us by His servants the prophets.
11 Yes, all Israel has transgressed Your law, and has departed so as not to obey Your voice; therefore the curse and the oath written in the Law of Moses the servant of God have been poured out on us, because we have sinned against Him.
12 And He has confirmed His words, which He spoke against us and against our judges who judged us, by bringing upon us a great disaster; for under the whole heaven such has never been done as what has been done to Jerusalem.
13 "As it is written in the Law of

Moses, all this disaster has come upon us; yet we have not made our prayer before the Lord our God, that we might turn from our iniquities and understand Your truth.

14 Therefore the Lord has kept the disaster in mind, and brought it upon us; for the Lord our God is righteous in all the works which He does, though we have not obeyed His voice.

15 And now, O Lord our God, who brought Your people out of the land of Egypt with a mighty hand, and made Yourself a name, as it is this day—we have sinned, we have done wickedly!

16 "O Lord, according to all Your righteousness, I pray, let Your anger and Your fury be turned away from Your city Jerusalem, Your holy mountain; because for our sins, and for the iniquities of our fathers, Jerusalem and Your people are a reproach to all those around us.

17 Now therefore, our God, hear the prayer of Your servant, and his supplications, and for the Lord's sake cause Your face to shine on Your sanctuary, which is desolate.

18 O my God, incline Your ear and hear; open Your eyes and see our desolations, and the city which is called by Your name; for we do not present our supplications before You because of our righteous deeds, but because of Your great mercies.

19 O Lord, hear! O Lord, forgive! O Lord, listen and act! Do not delay for Your own sake, my God, for Your city and Your people are called by Your name."

20 Now while I was speaking, praying, and confessing my sin and the sin of my people Israel, and presenting my supplication before the Lord my God for the holy mountain of my God,

21 yes, while I was speaking in prayer, the man Gabriel, whom I had seen in the vision at the beginning, being caused to fly swiftly, reached me about the time of the evening offering.

22 And he informed me, and talked with me, and said, "O Daniel, I have now come forth to give you skill to understand.

23 At the beginning of your supplications the command went out, and I have come to tell you, for you are greatly beloved; therefore consider the matter, and understand the vision:

24 "Seventy weeks are determined
For your people and for your holy
    city,
To finish the transgression,
To make an end of sins,
To make reconciliation for iniquity,
To bring in everlasting
    righteousness,
To seal up vision and prophecy,
And to anoint the Most Holy.

25 "Know therefore and understand,

That from the going forth of the command
To restore and build Jerusalem
Until Messiah the Prince,
There shall be seven weeks and sixty-two weeks;
The street shall be built again, and the wall,
Even in troublesome times.
26 "And after the sixty-two weeks
Messiah shall be cut off, but not for Himself;
And the people of the prince who is to come
Shall destroy the city and the sanctuary.
The end of it shall be with a flood,
And till the end of the war desolations are determined.
27 Then he shall confirm a covenant with many for one week;
But in the middle of the week
He shall bring an end to sacrifice and offering.
And on the wing of abominations shall be one who makes desolate,
Even until the consummation, which is determined,
Is poured out on the desolate."

CHAPTER 9

Unto Messiah the Prince

Inside this Chapter

Daniel 9:1–3 — Prophecy Fulfilled

"In the first year of Darius the son of Ahasuerus, of the lineage of the Medes, who was made king over the realm of the Chaldeans—in the first year of his reign I, Daniel, understood by the books the number of the years specified by the word of the Lord through Jeremiah the prophet, that He would accomplish seventy years in the desolations of Jerusalem.

Then I set my face toward the Lord God to make request by prayer and supplications, with fasting, sackcloth, and ashes."

Closer Look

The Time Had Come

Several years had passed since Daniel had seen the vision in chapter eight, and much had happened. Belshazzar had summoned him to read the handwriting on the wall; Belshazzar had been slain; and the Medes and Persians had taken over the kingdom. Daniel was appointed the foremost of three presidents over Medo-Persia, yet his people were uppermost in his mind. Jeremiah 25:11–12 and 29:10 both state the length of Israel's captivity. The time for their deliverance, foretold by God, had come. Now, with fasting and prayer, Daniel sought the explanation of the vision in chapter eight.

Daniel 9:4–19 — Daniel's Prayer

"And I prayed to the Lord my God, and made confession, and said, 'O Lord, great and awesome God, who keeps His covenant and mercy with those who love Him, and with those who keep His commandments, we have sinned and committed iniquity, we have done wickedly and rebelled, even by departing from Your precepts and Your judgments. Neither have we heeded Your servants the prophets, who spoke in Your name to our kings and our princes, to our fathers and all the people of the land. O Lord, righteousness belongs to You, but to us shame of face, as it is this day—to the men of Judah, to the inhabitants of Jerusalem and all Israel, those near and those far off in all the countries to which You have driven them, because of the unfaithfulness which they have committed against You.

"'O Lord, to us belongs shame of face, to our kings, our princes, and our fathers, because we have sinned against You. To the Lord our God belong mercy and forgiveness, though we have rebelled against Him. We have not obeyed the voice of the Lord our God, to walk in His laws, which He set before us by His servants the prophets. Yes, all Israel has transgressed Your

law, and has departed so as not to obey Your voice; therefore the curse and the oath written in the Law of Moses the servant of God have been poured out on us, because we have sinned against Him. And He has confirmed His words, which He spoke against us and against our judges who judged us, by bringing upon us a great disaster; for under the whole heaven such has never been done as what has been done to Jerusalem.

"As it is written in the Law of Moses, all this disaster has come upon us; yet we have not made our prayer before the Lord our God, that we might turn from our iniquities and understand Your truth. Therefore the Lord has kept the disaster in mind, and brought it upon us; for the Lord our God is righteous in all the works which He does, though we have not obeyed His voice. And now, O Lord our God, who brought Your people out of the land of Egypt with a mighty hand, and made Yourself a name, as it is this day—we have sinned, we have done wickedly!

"O Lord, according to all Your righteousness, I pray, let Your anger and Your fury be turned away from Your city Jerusalem, Your holy mountain; because for our sins, and for the iniquities of our fathers, Jerusalem and Your people are a reproach to all those around us. Now therefore, our God, hear the prayer of Your servant, and his supplications, and for the Lord's sake cause Your face to shine on Your sanctuary, which is desolate.

'O my God, incline Your ear and hear; open Your eyes and see our desolations, and the city which is called by Your name; for we do not present our supplications before You because of our righteous deeds, but because of Your great mercies. O Lord, hear! O Lord, forgive! O Lord, listen and act! Do not delay for Your own sake, my God, for Your city and Your people are called by Your name.'"

Infinite Love

Consider This

This is one of the greatest prayers recorded in Scripture, in which Daniel offered one of the most wonderful prayers on behalf of the children of Israel. Daniel understood the fallen condition of his people, and he confessed their sins to God. Yet this godly man, who was *"greatly beloved,"* identified himself with their sinfulness, placing himself on the same ground. Daniel knew that prayer and faith are the two arms that mortal man can wrap around the neck of Infinite Love. Clinging to God like Jacob of old, he claimed the promise, *"To the Lord our God belong mercy and forgiveness, though we have rebelled against*

Him. O Lord, according to all Your righteousness, I pray, let Your anger and Your fury be turned away from Your city Jerusalem … and for the Lord's sake cause Your face to shine on Your sanctuary." Daniel 8:9, 16–17.

Friend, this great and awesome God is still the same today.

Daniel 9:20–23 — The Angel Gabriel

"Now while I was speaking, praying, and confessing my sin and the sin of my people Israel, and presenting my supplication before the Lord my God for the holy mountain of my God, yes, while I was speaking in prayer, the man Gabriel, whom I had seen in the vision at the beginning, being caused to fly swiftly, reached me about the time of the evening offering. And he informed me, and talked with me, and said, 'O Daniel, I have now come forth to give you skill to understand. At the beginning of your supplications the command went out, and I have come to tell you, for you are greatly beloved; therefore consider the matter, and understand the vision.'"

Closer Look

Who Is Gabriel?

Gabriel is one of the myriad angels in the courts of Heaven; and one of the two cherubim who stand in the throne room of God, in His very presence (see Exodus 25:18-20). Gabriel interpreted the visions for Daniel, and explained when the Messiah would appear. Six hundred years later, this same angel visited Zacharias concerning the birth of John the Baptist, and later talked with Mary about the fulfillment of the prophecy concerning the Messiah and Jesus' birth. Gabriel explained to Daniel one of the most marvelous prophecies in Scripture. Anyone who studies these prophecies with an open mind will recognize that Jesus Christ is the Messiah, the only One who fulfills what was foretold.

Daniel 9:24–27 — Seventy-Week Prophecy

"Seventy weeks are determined
For your people and for your holy city,
To finish the transgression,
To make an end of sins,
To make reconciliation for iniquity,
To bring in everlasting righteousness,

To seal up vision and prophecy,
And to anoint the Most Holy.
Know therefore and understand,
That from the going forth of the command
To restore and build Jerusalem
Until Messiah the Prince,
There shall be seven weeks and sixty-two weeks;
The street shall be built again, and the wall,
Even in troublesome times.
And after the sixty-two weeks
Messiah shall be cut off, but not for Himself;
And the people of the prince who is to come
Shall destroy the city and the sanctuary.
The end of it shall be with a flood,
And till the end of the war desolations are determined.
Then he shall confirm a covenant with many for one week;
But in the middle of the week
He shall bring an end to sacrifice and offering.
And on the wing of abominations shall be one who makes desolate,
Even until the consummation, which is determined,
Is poured out on the desolate."

2,300 Days

Remember that it was the 2,300 days of chapter eight, verses 13 and 14, that Daniel did not understand. Therefore, to separate the 70 weeks from the 2,300 days does not give a complete picture. God has given us an essential rule to help us understand prophecies which deal with time, i.e., in prophecy, one prophetic day represents one literal year: *"I have laid on you a day for each year."* Ezekiel 4:6. *"For each day you shall bear your guilt one year."* Numbers 14:34. God uses His crucial day-for-a-year principle extensively in the books of Daniel and Revelation.

The day-for-a-year principle has been recognized by Bible students down through the ages, and supporters of this principle include theologians such as Augustine, Tychonius, Andreas, Ambrosius, Ansbertus, Berengaud, and the leading modern expositors.

However, the most convincing fact is that the prophecies have been precisely fulfilled based on this principle. You will find this to be true with the prophecies of Daniel 7 and 9, as well as those in Revelation 11, 12, and 13.

How do we know that this principal of interpreting prophecy is correct? Very simply, because it works. Watch carefully how perfectly it unveils the events that were to take place:

First Event: *Seventy Weeks*

"Seventy weeks are determined For your people and for your holy city." Daniel 9:24.

The original Hebrew text states, "Seventy weeks are 'cut off' for your people, meaning the 70 weeks / 490 years are part of the 2,300 days / years God set aside (cut off) for a specific purpose. The 70 weeks / 490 years is the time God allotted the Jewish people to change their ways, *"to finish the transgression, to make an end of sins;"* in other words, to return to Him and be His people, to walk in His ways, and to obey His voice.

In the ancient Sanctuary service, God had provided all the provisions necessary for the Jewish people *"to make reconciliation for iniquity."* In the final week of the 70 week / 490 year prophecy, Christ would come *"to bring in everlasting righteousness,"* and His righteousness would be preached to the entire world.

The sinless life of Christ, His anointing at His baptism, and the time of His death would *"seal up vision and prophecy,"* showing that He is the Blessed Hope of All Ages, the Messiah, the Prince. By the end of the 70 prophetic weeks, the fulfillment of all the specifications in the prophecy would seal the authenticity of the vision.

Second Event: *Know and Understand*

"Know therefore and understand." Daniel 9:25.

Gabriel now begins to explain the 70 prophetic weeks / 490 literal years in detail.

At this time, Jerusalem lies in ruins: *"That from the going forth of the command to restore and build Jerusalem."* Daniel 9:25. There were three decrees given to restore and rebuild Jerusalem. The book of Ezra records them all:

Cyrus gave a decree in 538 B.C., allowing the Jewish exiles to return to their homeland (Ezra 1:2–4). They took back with them the sacred vessels Nebuchadnezzar had taken from the temple. Zerubbabel led approximately 50,000 exiles on this return.

Darius I, also known as Darius the Great, gave a second decree in 519 B.C., confirming the original decree made by Cyrus (Ezra 6:6–12).

The final decree was made by Artaxerxes (Ezra 7:11–26). It was this decree that gave Jerusalem its legal rebirth, for Artaxerxes authorized Ezra to return with another group of exiles, and to appoint magistrates and judges. This took place in the autumn of 457 B.C.

Ezra 6:14 makes clear that all three decrees are required in order to constitute the commands of Daniel 9:25: *"And they built and finished it, ... according to the command of Cyrus, Darius, and Artaxerxes king of Persia."* Since these three decrees are connected, the starting date for the prophecy would be 457 B.C.

Third Event: *Three-Part Division*
Three time segments make up the 70 weeks / 490 years given by Gabriel.

Using the day-for-a-year principle:

Segment 1	Segment 2	Segment 3	Total
"There shall be seven weeks" (Daniel 9:25)	"and sixty-two weeks" (Daniel 9:25)	"Then he shall confirm a covenant with many for one week" (Daniel 9:27)	
7 weeks to rebuild Jerusalem =	62 additional weeks unto the Messiah=	1 week in confirming the covenant=	70 Weeks
49 years	434 years	7 years	490 Years

Let's examine this prophecy, beginning at our starting point of 457 B.C.

"Until Messiah the Prince, there shall be seven weeks and sixty-two weeks" (Daniel 9:25). Applying the day-for-a-year principle, 7 plus 62 equals 69 prophetic weeks; multiplying 69 weeks times 7 days per week gives us 483 literal years. Artaxerxes' decree was given in 457 B.C., and adding 483 years to 457 B.C. brings us to the fall of 27 A.D. They did not utilize a "year zero" when the transition was made from B.C. to A.D.;

therefore, since A.D. started with year 1, not 0, remember to add one year when making this computation.

Let's examine this prophecy, beginning at our starting point of 457 B.C.

"Until Messiah the Prince, there shall be seven weeks and sixty-two weeks" Daniel 9:25.

Luke 3:1 records what happened at that time: *"Now in the fifteenth year of the reign of Tiberius Caesar ..."* secular history records the fifteenth year of Tiberius Caesar, as 27 A.D.

Luke continues: *"When all the people were baptized, it came to pass that Jesus also was baptized; and while He prayed, the heaven was opened. And the Holy Spirit descended in bodily form like a dove upon Him, and a voice came from heaven which said, 'You are My beloved Son; in You I am well pleased.' Now Jesus Himself began His ministry at about thirty years of age."* Luke 3:21–23.

Exactly as the angel Gabriel had foretold, it would be 483 years *"until Messiah the Prince."* Daniel 9:25. Jesus appeared exactly on time! No one but Jesus of Nazareth fits the time, or the place. Each person who is intellectually honest must weigh these facts and decide for himself whether Jesus is the Messiah, the Savior of the world.

Fourth Event: *Messiah Cut Off*

We have already addressed the *"seven weeks and sixty-two weeks"* of Daniel 9:25; the 483 years which led us to Jesus' baptism, and the beginning of His public ministry. The following verse, Daniel 9:26, details what would happen after the 483 years, i.e., after Jesus' baptism: *"And after the sixty-two weeks Messiah shall be cut off, but not for Himself; And the people of the prince who is to come shall destroy the city and the sanctuary."* The *"sixty-two weeks"* begins after the *"seven weeks"* that was given to restore and build Jerusalem.

The rebuilding of the walls and city of Jerusalem occurred during the first *"seven weeks"* or 49 years of the 69 week / 483 year period. Gabriel said the Messiah would be cut off, and the city and sanctuary (temple) would be destroyed, *"after the sixty-two weeks"* which followed, i.e., sometime after the 7 + 62 weeks / 483 years leading to Jesus' baptism. Please note this passage does not state that the city and the sanctuary would be destroyed within the 70 weeks / 490 years that God set aside for the Jews; it states that it would occur after the 62 weeks, i.e., sometime after the baptism of Jesus.

This was a contention between Jesus and the Pharisees. Concerning the temple, Jesus said, *"Not one stone shall be left here upon another."* Matthew 24:2. Secular history records that the Roman general Titus destroyed both the temple, and the city of Jerusalem, in 70 A.D., i.e., after the 62 weeks, just as the prophecy—and Jesus—had foretold.

Fifth Event: *Confirm a Covenant*

"Then He shall confirm a covenant with many for one week." Daniel 9:26.

The 7 and 62 weeks / 483 years ended in 27 A.D., at the baptism of Jesus. At that time, the Holy Spirit descended upon Him in the form of a dove, confirming God's approval from Heaven. This marked the beginning of His ministry. Of the 70 weeks God had allowed the Jewish people, only one week remained.

Adding one week, or 7 years, to 27 A.D. brings us to 34 A.D. *"But in the middle of the week, He shall bring an end to sacrifice and offering."* Daniel 9:26. Three and one-half years after Jesus' baptism, in the middle of the prophetic week, the very ones Christ tried to save cut Him off, crucifying Him at the time of the Passover feast, in the spring of 31 A.D. When Jesus had breathed His last, the inner veil in the temple was miraculously torn in two from top to bottom, revealing the Most Holy Place in which the ark with the mercy seat, and the Shekinah Glory of God, had dwelt.

God had withdrawn His presence from the temple. The Lamb of God had been slain, and the *"sacrifice and offering"* were abolished forever, leaving the last half of the final week of God's 70 week / 490 years, to be fulfilled. The Holy Spirit was poured out upon the disciples, and for another three and one-half years they labored to convert the Jewish people with the gospel of Jesus Christ.

This final three and one-half years of the 70 week portion of the 2,300 day / year prophecy ended with an act of defiance in 34 A.D. That is when the Jewish leaders stoned Stephen, the first Christian martyr, to death. The stoning of Stephen occurred exactly 70 weeks / 490 years after Artaxerxes' decree for the Jewish people to return to Jerusalem.

The Scripture is clear that the Jewish people were to have been a light to the Gentiles, but they had failed to accomplish their trust. Since the Jewish people had not returned to God by doing what He had asked of them, the gospel went to the Gentiles: *"Then Paul and Barnabas grew* bold and said, 'It was necessary that the word of God should be spoken to you [the Jews] first; but since you reject it, and judge yourselves unworthy of everlasting life, behold, we turn to the Gentiles.' (Acts 13:46).

Two events recorded in Scripture mark the execution of God's plan to take the gospel to the Gentiles. Chapter 9 of the book of Acts records the conversion of Saul of Tarsus. In Acts 22:21, Jesus said to him, *"Depart for I will send you far from here to the Gentiles."* Saul, later called Paul, was converted a short time after he witnessed the stoning of Stephen, and he subsequently took the gospel to the Gentiles.

The other event is in Acts 10. Peter was praying when he saw a sheet descending toward him from heaven, full of unclean animals. He then heard a voice saying, *"Rise, Peter; kill and eat"* (Acts 10:13), to which he responded, *"Not so, Lord! For I have never eaten anything common or unclean"* (verse 14).

Later, at the home of the Roman soldier Cornelius, Peter explained what the vision meant: *"Then he said to them, 'You know how unlawful it is for a Jewish man to keep company with or go to one of another nation. But God has shown me that I should not call any man common or unclean'"* (Acts 10:28). These events occurred in 34 A.D., which is when the gospel went to the Gentiles.

"And on the wing of abominations shall be one who makes desolate ..." Daniel 9:27. Less than forty years later, in 70 A.D., the pagan Roman army would make the temple and city of Jerusalem desolate, *"until the consummation"* of all things, at the time *"determined."*

Sixth Event: *Sanctuary Shall Be Cleansed*

To complete the 2,300 day / year prophecy, we have to go back to Gabriel's message to Daniel, "For two thousand three hundred days; then the sanctuary shall be cleansed" (Daniel 8:14). The Scripture separates the 70 weeks / 490 years we have already covered, from the total of 2,300 days / years. By subtracting 490 from 2,300, we are left with 1,810 years. Using the day-for-a-year principle, when we add 1,810 years to 34 A.D. *the end of the 70 weeks / 490 years, we come to 1844 A.D. At this time, "the sanctuary shall be cleansed."* Daniel 8:14.

The phrase, "cleansing of the sanctuary," refers to the Day of Atonement, also known as the Day of Judgment. Today, the Jewish people refer to it as Yom Kippur. The word "sanctuary" also means "temple," and since this prophecy speaks of the sanctuary being cleansed in 1844 A.D., it cannot be speaking of the temple in Jerusalem, because it was destroyed in 70 A.D. The books of Hebrews and Revelation are both very clear about a temple (sanctuary) in Heaven. Hebrews 8:5 tells us that the sanctuary on earth was only a pattern of the one in Heaven, where Christ is now ministering for us as our High Priest.

The High Priest entered the Most Holy Place of the earthly sanctuary/ temple only once each year, on the annual Day of Atonement. He would take the blood of the sacrificial goat, make his way through the first compartment of the temple (the Holy Place), part the inner veil which separated the temple's two compartments, and step into the second compartment, the Most Holy Place, to appear in the very presence of God. He would then sprinkle the blood on the Mercy Seat, confessing, and asking forgiveness for the sins of Israel committed during the past year. This was a day of judgment, and of cleansing the earthly sanctuary/ temple of all sin, giving the people a fresh start.

Daniel 7 pictures this cleansing of the true sanctuary in Heaven: *"I watched till thrones were put in place, and the Ancient of Days was seated.... The court was seated, and the books were opened."* Daniel 7:9–10.

"One like the Son of Man, coming with the clouds of heaven! He came to the Ancient of Days... and a judgment was made in favor of the saints of the Most High." Daniel 7:13, 22.

This is a picture of the Ancient of Days (God the Father), taking a seat, and opening the books, which contain the record of each person's life. The Son of Man (Jesus) comes to His Father with the angels, "the clouds of heaven," and judgment is made in favor of the saints. Because of the blood of the Lamb of God, sins are forgiven, and the record is cleansed. This is Gabriel's explanation of Daniel 8 and 9. The cleansing of the heavenly sanctuary began in 1844 A.D., and it will end when Jesus returns to set up His eternal kingdom.

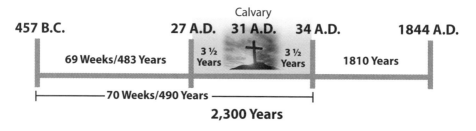

DANIEL 10

1 In the third year of Cyrus king of Persia a message was revealed to Daniel, whose name was called Belteshazzar. The message was true, but the appointed time was long; and he understood the message, and had understanding of the vision.

2 In those days I, Daniel, was mourning three full weeks.

3 I ate no pleasant food, no meat or wine came into my mouth, nor did I anoint myself at all, till three whole weeks were fulfilled.

4 Now on the twenty-fourth day of the first month, as I was by the side of the great river, that is, the Tigris,

5 I lifted my eyes and looked, and behold, a certain man clothed in linen, whose waist was girded with gold of Uphaz!

6 His body was like beryl, his face like the appearance of lightning, his eyes like torches of fire, his arms and feet like burnished bronze in color, and the sound of his words like the voice of a multitude.

7 And I, Daniel, alone saw the vision, for the men who were with me did not see the vision; but a great terror fell upon them, so that they fled to hide themselves.

8 Therefore I was left alone when I saw this great vision, and no strength remained in me; for my vigor was turned to frailty in me, and I retained no strength.

9 Yet I heard the sound of his words; and while I heard the sound of his words I was in a deep sleep on my face, with my face to the ground.

10 Suddenly, a hand touched me, which made me tremble on my knees and on the palms of my hands.

11 And he said to me, "O Daniel, man greatly beloved, understand the words that I speak to you, and stand upright, for I have now been sent to you." While he was speaking this word to me, I stood trembling.

12 Then he said to me, "Do not fear, Daniel, for from the first day that you set your heart to understand, and to humble yourself before your God, your words were heard; and I have come because of your words.

13 But the prince of the kingdom of Persia withstood me twenty-one days; and behold, Michael, one of the chief princes, came to help me, for I had been left alone there with the kings of Persia.

14 Now I have come to make you understand what will happen to your people in the latter days, for the vision refers to many days yet to come."

15 When he had spoken such words to me, I turned my face

toward the ground and became speechless.

16 And suddenly, one having the likeness of the sons of men touched my lips; then I opened my mouth and spoke, saying to him who stood before me, "My lord, because of the vision my sorrows have overwhelmed me, and I have retained no strength.

17 For how can this servant of my lord talk with you, my lord? As for me, no strength remains in me now, nor is any breath left in me."

18 Then again, the one having the likeness of a man touched me and strengthened me.

19 And he said, "O man greatly beloved, fear not! Peace be to you; be strong, yes, be strong!"

So when he spoke to me I was strengthened, and said, "Let my lord speak, for you have strengthened me."

20 Then he said, "Do you know why I have come to you? And now I must return to fight with the prince of Persia; and when I have gone forth, indeed the prince of Greece will come.

21 But I will tell you what is noted in the Scripture of Truth. (No one upholds me against these, except Michael your prince.

CHAPTER 10

Visitors from Heaven

Inside this Chapter

Daniel 10:1–3 — Daniel's Burden

"In the third year of Cyrus king of Persia a message was revealed to Daniel, whose name was called Belteshazzar. The message was true, but the appointed time was long; and he understood the message, and had understanding of the vision. In those days I, Daniel, was mourning three full weeks. I ate no pleasant food, no meat or wine came into my mouth, nor did I anoint myself at all, till three whole weeks were fulfilled."

King of Persia

Daniel's fasting and mourning were due to the events affecting the Jewish people. At that time, the opposition by the Samaritans against the Jews who had returned to Jerusalem weighed heavily on Daniel's mind. Zerubbabel had just returned from Jerusalem, and had given a report of the Jew's progress there. However, due to false reports that the Samaritans had sent back to Persia, there was a serious threat that Cyrus' decree for the children of Israel to return to Jerusalem, and to rebuild it, might not be carried to completion.

The conflict that occurred is recorded in verse 13. For three weeks, the angel Gabriel had grappled with the powers of darkness; struggling to nullify Satan's work on the mind of the king of Persia. Through this great conflict, the victory was gained, and the forces of evil were restrained during the lifetimes of Cyrus, and his son, Cambyses.

Daniel 10:4–9 — Daniel's Vision of Christ

"Now on the twenty-fourth day of the first month, as I was by the side of the great river, that is, the Tigris, I lifted my eyes and looked, and behold, a certain man clothed in linen, whose waist was girded with gold of Uphaz! His body was like beryl, his face like the appearance of lightning, his eyes like torches of fire, his arms and feet like burnished bronze in color, and the sound of his words like the voice of a multitude.

"And I, Daniel, alone saw the vision, for the men who were with me did not see the vision; but a great terror fell upon them, so that they fled to hide themselves. Therefore I was left alone when I saw this great vision, and no strength remained in me; for my vigor was turned to frailty in me, and I retained no strength. Yet I heard the sound of his words; and while I heard the sound of his words I was in a deep sleep on my face, with my face to the ground."

Christ in the Old and New Testaments

This vision which Daniel was given beside the Tigris (or Hiddekel) River, is almost identical to the description of Christ that John was given in Revelation 1:13–16.

It is interesting to note that this description of Christ was recorded centuries before Mary gave birth to Him, and before He took on the nature of man. In Revelation, John gives a description of Christ after His resurrection, and ascension to Heaven. Both descriptions are similar, except that John mentions His white hair.

Daniel describes the body of Jesus as being like beryl, which was one of the stones used in the breastplate of the High Priest. His priestly garment of linen was that of a King, and a High Priest, for Jesus fills both offices. The gold around His waist also identified Him as a king.

Daniel 10:10–12 — The Touch of an Angel

"Suddenly, a hand touched me, which made me tremble on my knees and on the palms of my hands. And he said to me, 'O Daniel, man greatly beloved, understand the words that I speak to you, and stand upright, for I have now been sent to you.' While he was speaking this word to me, I stood trembling.

"Then he said to me, 'Do not fear, Daniel, for from the first day that you set your heart to understand, and to humble yourself before your God, your words were heard; and I have come because of your words.'"

Gabriel

Gabriel, who had so faithfully ministered to Daniel, reached out and touched him as he lay flat on the ground. With the power of that touch, Daniel got up, trembling, on his hands and knees. He then heard these reassuring words, *"O Daniel, man greatly beloved, stand upright."* His prayer had been heard.

Daniel 10:13 — Michael

"But the prince of the kingdom of Persia withstood me twenty-one days; and behold, Michael, one of the chief princes, came to help me, for I had been left alone there with the kings of Persia."

Who is Michael?

In Hebrew, the name Michael means, *"Who is like God?"*

Several times, Daniel referred to Michael as the Prince:

"At that time Michael shall stand up, The great prince* who stands watch over the sons of your people." Daniel 12:1.

"But the prince of the kingdom of Persia withstood me twenty-one days; and behold, Michael, one of the chief princes*, came to help me, for I had been left alone there with the kings of Persia." Daniel 10:13.

"But I will tell you what is noted in the Scripture of Truth. (No one upholds me against these, except Michael your prince*)." Daniel 10:21.

Daniel and other Bible writers assign the title of "Prince" to Christ.

"Know therefore and understand, that from the going forth of the command to restore and build Jerusalem until Messiah the Prince*..." Daniel 9:25.

"For unto us a Child is born, unto us a Son is given; and the government will be upon His shoulder. And His name will be called Wonderful, Counselor, Mighty God, Everlasting Father, Prince* of Peace." Isaiah 9:6.

"Him God has exalted to His right hand to be Prince* and Savior, to give repentance to Israel and forgiveness of sins." Acts 5:31. **Emphasis provided.*

In the book of Jude, the Bible speaks of Michael as the Archangel, *"Yet Michael the archangel, in contending with the devil, when he disputed about the body of Moses, dared not bring against him a reviling accusation, but said, 'The Lord rebuke you!' "* Jude 1:9. *"Michael the archangel"* clearly refers to Christ, because no angel, or other being, has the power to resurrect the dead. Here, for the first time, Christ exercised His power as Creator and Redeemer in calling Moses from the dead.

The Apostle Paul, in describing the first resurrection, i.e., the resurrection of the redeemed at Christ's second coming, also speaks of the Archangel calling His people from the grave: *"For the Lord Himself will descend from heaven with a shout, with the voice of an archangel, and with the trumpet of God. And the dead in Christ will rise first."* 1 Thessalonians 4:16.

In Hebrew, the word for Prince is "Sar," and the same word is used for Commander. Notice this interesting conversation, recorded in the book of Joshua: *"And it came to pass, when Joshua was by Jericho, that he lifted his eyes and looked, and behold, a Man stood opposite him with His sword drawn in His hand. And Joshua went to Him and said to Him, 'Are You for us or for our adversaries?' So He said, 'No, but as Commander of the army of the Lord I have now come.' And Joshua fell on his face to the earth and worshiped, and said to Him, 'What does my Lord say to His servant?' Then the Commander of the Lord's army said to Joshua, 'Take your sandal off your foot, for the place where you stand is holy.' And Joshua did so."* Joshua 5:13–15.

Several exchanges in this dialogue reflect the fact that this was Christ, and not an angel: Joshua falling on his face and worshiping. He referred to the Commander as Lord; and told to take off his shoes, for the ground was holy. Exodus 5:13–55.

Jesus' statement that He is Commander of the Lord's army is like the president of the United States saying that he is Commander in Chief of the Armed Forces. Just as a person doesn't have to be a soldier to be the Commander, so Christ does not have to be an angel to be the Commander. Michael the Prince, the Archangel, and the Commander of the Lord's army, is our Savior and Redeemer.

Daniel 10:14–17 — Frailty of Mankind

"'Now I have come to make you understand what will happen to your people in the latter days, for the vision refers to many days yet to come.'

When he had spoken such words to me, I turned my face toward the ground and became speechless. And suddenly, one having the likeness of the sons of men touched my lips; then I opened my mouth and spoke, saying to him who stood before me, 'My lord, because of the vision my sorrows have overwhelmed me, and I have retained no strength. For how can this servant of my lord talk with you, my lord? As for me, no strength remains in me now, nor is any breath left in me.'"

Retained No Strength

How little we understand our frailty. As Gabriel spoke to Daniel about what would happen to the followers of the Lord in the last days, Daniel was overwhelmed by the greatness and power of God. A sense of his own deficiency filled his mind, and he was profoundly humbled by the sense of his own unworthiness. As he beheld the glory and majesty of the heavenly messenger, his strength left him, and he was speechless. All who encounter Jesus lose any pretense of self-righteousness, nor do they wrap themselves in a garb of holiness; instead, pride and egotism are discarded. By seeking the righteousness of Christ, they desire to be like Him in character.

Daniel 10:18–21 — Strengthened by an Angel

"Then again, the one having the likeness of a man touched me and strengthened me. And he said, 'O man greatly beloved, fear not! Peace be to you; be strong, yes, be strong!'

"So when he spoke to me I was strengthened, and said, 'Let my lord speak, for you have strengthened me.'

"Then he said, 'Do you know why I have come to you? And now I must return to fight with the prince of Persia; and when I have gone forth, indeed the prince of Greece will come. But I will tell you what is noted in the Scripture of Truth. (No one upholds me against these, except Michael your prince.)'"

Consider This

Greatly Beloved

Three times, Daniel was told that he was greatly beloved. His was a life of total commitment to God. Even though he confessed his sins in chapter 9, Scripture records no incident in which he ever did wrong.

The phrase *"fight with the prince of Persia"* does not mean to fight against him, but beside him, or on his behalf. Men and women like Daniel, Ezra, Esther, Nehemiah, Haggai, and Zechariah were a strong witness to the nation of Persia. As long as the nation worked for God and His people, the powers of Heaven were on the side of the Persians. However, Persia eventually lost its direction, so that Christ and the angel Gabriel stopped working on its behalf: *"... when I have gone forth."* It was time for the next kingdom to arise, as Persia left the scene of action.

In Daniel 2, 7, and 8, it was foretold that Greece would be the next power to dominate the then-known world.

In chapter 10, Gabriel led up to the events that transpire in Daniel 11, and 12.

DANIEL 11

1 "Also in the first year of Darius the Mede, I, even I, stood up to confirm and strengthen him.)

2 And now I will tell you the truth: Behold, three more kings will arise in Persia, and the fourth shall be far richer than them all; by his strength, through his riches, he shall stir up all against the realm of Greece.

3 Then a mighty king shall arise, who shall rule with great dominion, and do according to his will.

4 And when he has arisen, his kingdom shall be broken up and divided toward the four winds of heaven, but not among his posterity nor according to his dominion with which he ruled; for his kingdom shall be uprooted, even for others besides these.

5 "Also the king of the South shall become strong, as well as one of his princes; and he shall gain power over him and have dominion. His dominion shall be a great dominion.

6 And at the end of some years they shall join forces, for the daughter of the king of the South shall go to the king of the North to make an agreement; but she shall not retain the power of her authority, and neither he nor his authority shall stand; but she shall be given up, with those who brought her, and with him who begot her, and with him who strengthened her in those times.

7 But from a branch of her roots one shall arise in his place, who shall come with an army, enter the fortress of the king of the North, and deal with them and prevail.

8 And he shall also carry their gods captive to Egypt, with their princes and their precious articles of silver and gold; and he shall continue more years than the king of the North.

9 "Also the king of the North shall come to the kingdom of the king of the South, but shall return to his own land.

10 However his sons shall stir up strife, and assemble a multitude of great forces; and one shall certainly come and overwhelm and pass through; then he shall return to his fortress and stir up strife.

11 "And the king of the South shall be moved with rage, and go out and fight with him, with the king of the North, who shall muster a great multitude; but the multitude shall be given into the hand of his enemy.

12 When he has taken away the multitude, his heart will be lifted

up; and he will cast down tens of thousands, but he will not prevail.

13 For the king of the North will return and muster a multitude greater than the former, and shall certainly come at the end of some years with a great army and much equipment.

14 "Now in those times many shall rise up against the king of the South. Also, violent men of your people shall exalt themselves in fulfillment of the vision, but they shall fall.

15 So the king of the North shall come and build a siege mound, and take a fortified city; and the forces of the South shall not withstand him. Even his choice troops shall have no strength to resist.

16 But he who comes against him shall do according to his own will, and no one shall stand against him. He shall stand in the Glorious Land with destruction in his power.

17 "He shall also set his face to enter with the strength of his whole kingdom, and upright ones with him; thus shall he do. And he shall give him the daughter of women to destroy it; but she shall not stand with him, or be for him.

18 After this he shall turn his face to the coastlands, and shall take many. But a ruler shall bring the reproach against them to an end; and with the reproach removed, he shall turn back on him.

19 Then he shall turn his face toward the fortress of his own land; but he shall stumble and fall, and not be found.

20 "There shall arise in his place one who imposes taxes on the glorious kingdom; but within a few days he shall be destroyed, but not in anger or in battle.

21 And in his place shall arise a vile person, to whom they will not give the honor of royalty; but he shall come in peaceably, and seize the kingdom by intrigue.

22 With the force of a flood they shall be swept away from before him and be broken, and also the prince of the covenant.

23 And after the league is made with him he shall act deceitfully, for he shall come up and become strong with a small number of people.

24 He shall enter peaceably, even into the richest places of the province; and he shall do what his fathers have not done, nor his forefathers: he shall disperse among them the plunder, spoil, and riches; and he shall devise his plans against the strongholds, but only for a time.

25 "He shall stir up his power and his courage against the king of the South with a great army. And the king of the South shall be stirred up to battle with a very great and mighty army; but he shall not stand,

for they shall devise plans against him.

26 Yes, those who eat of the portion of his delicacies shall destroy him; his army shall be swept away, and many shall fall down slain.

27 Both these kings' hearts shall be bent on evil, and they shall speak lies at the same table; but it shall not prosper, for the end will still be at the appointed time.

28 While returning to his land with great riches, his heart shall be moved against the holy covenant; so he shall do damage and return to his own land.

29 "At the appointed time he shall return and go toward the south; but it shall not be like the former or the latter.

30 For ships from Cyprus shall come against him; therefore he shall be grieved, and return in rage against the holy covenant, and do damage.

"So he shall return and show regard for those who forsake the holy covenant.

31 And forces shall be mustered by him, and they shall defile the sanctuary fortress; then they shall take away the daily sacrifices, and place there the abomination of desolation.

32 Those who do wickedly against the covenant he shall corrupt with flattery; but the people who know their God shall be strong, and carry out great exploits.

33 And those of the people who understand shall instruct many; yet for many days they shall fall by sword and flame, by captivity and plundering.

34 Now when they fall, they shall be aided with a little help; but many shall join with them by intrigue.

35 And some of those of understanding shall fall, to refine them, purify them, and make them white, until the time of the end; because it is still for the appointed time.

36 "Then the king shall do according to his own will: he shall exalt and magnify himself above every god, shall speak blasphemies against the God of gods, and shall prosper till the wrath has been accomplished; for what has been determined shall be done.

37 He shall regard neither the God of his fathers nor the desire of women, nor regard any god; for he shall exalt himself above them all.

38 But in their place he shall honor a god of fortresses; and a god which his fathers did not know he shall honor with gold and silver, with precious stones and pleasant things.

39 Thus he shall act against the strongest fortresses with a foreign god, which he shall acknowledge, and advance its glory; and he shall cause them to rule over many, and divide the land for gain.

40 "At the time of the end the king

of the South shall attack him; and the king of the North shall come against him like a whirlwind, with chariots, horsemen, and with many ships; and he shall enter the countries, overwhelm them, and pass through.

41 He shall also enter the Glorious Land, and many countries shall be overthrown; but these shall escape from his hand: Edom, Moab, and the prominent people of Ammon. **42** He shall stretch out his hand against the countries, and the land of Egypt shall not escape. **43** He shall have power over the treasures of gold and silver, and over all the precious things of Egypt; also the Libyans and Ethiopians shall follow at his heels. **44** But news from the east and the north shall trouble him; therefore he shall go out with great fury to destroy and annihilate many. **45** And he shall plant the tents of his palace between the seas and the glorious holy mountain; yet he shall come to his end, and no one will help him.

CHAPTER 11

Outline of the World From Daniel's Day to Our Day

Inside this Chapter

Daniel 11:1–2 — *History of Persia*

"Also in the first year of Darius the Mede, I, even I, stood up to confirm and strengthen him. And now I will tell you the truth: Behold, three more kings will arise in Persia, and the fourth shall be far richer than them all; by his strength, through his riches, he shall stir up all against the realm of Greece."

I Will Tell You the Truth

Just as kingdoms are built by the power and prowess of men who age and die; nations also rise and pass away. Throughout the book of Daniel, the Bible consistently mentions four kingdoms: Babylon, Medo-Persia, Greece, and Rome. Since Babylon had now fallen, the angel Gabriel begins with the kingdom of Persia. Although he mentions several kings, he is referring to the kingdom of Persia in each case.

As the chapter progresses through the kingdoms to Greece and Pagan Rome, it follows the same format. However, Gabriel emphasizes Papal Rome as the king in verses 30–39, and he refers to it as the king of the North in verses 40–45.

Darius the Mede was the first king of Medo-Persia, the united kingdom of the Medes and Persians. Since he was advanced in age when he took the throne, he only reigned two years before his death. His nephew Cyrus then took the throne, and the explanation Gabriel gave Daniel occurred in the third year of his reign:

"Behold, three more kings will arise in Persia." Daniel 11:2.

After the death of Cyrus, the next three kings were:

- Cambyses, his son, who was Ahasuerus of Ezra 4:6 (530–522 B.C.)
- Bardiya, (called the False Smerdis), an impostor who took the throne. He was the Artaxerxes of Ezra 4:7, and ruled only seven months (522 B.C.)
- Darius the Persian, spoken of in Ezra 4:24, was Darius I (522-486 BC). Cyrus and Darius both issued decrees to rebuild the temple.

"And the fourth shall be far richer than them all; by his strength, through his riches, he shall stir up all against the realm of Greece."

The fourth king of Medo-Persia was Xerxes, known in the Bible as

Ahasuerus, the husband of Queen Esther (520-465 B.C.). He inherited immense riches, and established the largest army in history.

Artaxerxes Longimanus, the successor of Xerxes, issued the final decree for the return of the Jews to Judah, in 457 B.C. The Medo-Persian Empire reached its zenith during his reign, but neither man, nor nation, has ever, been able to handle wealth. Probation passed for another nation; as the Persian kingdom sank into a state of weakness, and the angel withdrew its sheltering wings, Greece was knocking at its door.

Daniel 11:3–13 — History of Greece

"Then a mighty king shall arise, who shall rule with great dominion, and do according to his will. And when he has arisen, his kingdom shall be broken up and divided toward the four winds of heaven, but not among his posterity nor according to his dominion with which he ruled; for his kingdom shall be uprooted, even for others besides these.

"Also the king of the South shall become strong, as well as one of his princes; and he shall gain power over him and have dominion. His dominion shall be a great dominion. And at the end of some years they shall join forces, for the daughter of the king of the South shall go to the king of the North to make an agreement; but she shall not retain the power of her authority, and neither he nor his authority shall stand; but she shall be given up, with those who brought her, and with him who begot her, and with him who strengthened her in those times. But from a branch of her roots one shall arise in his place, who shall come with an army, enter the fortress of the king of the North, and deal with them and prevail. And he shall also carry their gods captive to Egypt, with their princes and their precious articles of silver and gold; and he shall continue more years than the king of the North.

"Also the king of the North shall come to the kingdom of the king of the South, but shall return to his own land. However his sons shall stir up strife, and assemble a multitude of great forces; and one shall certainly come and overwhelm and pass through; then he shall return to his fortress and stir up strife.

"And the king of the South shall be moved with rage, and go out and fight with him, with the king of the North, who shall muster a great multitude; but the multitude shall be given into the hand of his enemy. When he has taken away the multitude, his heart will be lifted up; and he will cast down

tens of thousands, but he will not prevail. For the king of the North will return and muster a multitude greater than the former, and shall certainly come at the end of some years with a great army and much equipment."

A Mighty King Shall Arise

During his last meeting with Daniel, the angel Gabriel set aside the symbolic language of previous chapters in order to be unmistakably clear. He presented to Daniel the history of Medo-Persia, Greece, and Rome in plain and literal language. In this way, Alexander the Great was introduced, *"Then a mighty king shall arise."* Daniel 11:3.

Alexander was not a Greek, but a Macedonian—the son of Philip, the king of Macedon. Educated by Aristotle, and a pupil of Plato, he was taught the wisdom, language, and culture of the Greeks. When Philip died, he left the government to Alexander, who was twenty years old. In eight short years, Alexander enlarged his kingdom to include Asia Minor, Babylon, Egypt, and India. As the Scripture states, *"who shall rule with great dominion, and do according to his will."* Daniel 11:3. After reaching the pinnacle of his success, Alexander died on a banquet table in Babylon at the young age of 33, following two days of unrestrained drinking, and an attack of malaria fever.

"And when he has arisen, his kingdom shall be broken up and divided toward the four winds of heaven." Daniel 11:4.

After the death of Alexander, eight of his generals contended for his empire, but none were strong enough to gain supremacy. Finally, after twenty years of war and contention, his kingdom was divided between his four strongest generals: Ptolemy ruled Egypt, Seleucus controlled Syria and the east, Lysimachus held power over Thrace and Asia Minor, and Cassander ruled Greece.

Alexander's kingdom was divided, *"but not among his posterity nor according to his dominion with which he ruled; for his kingdom shall be uprooted, even for others besides these."* Daniel 11:4. Within fifteen years after his death, not one of his posterity remained alive; Alexander's family had become extinct.

The division of the kingdom into four parts was short-lived, because the four generals turned on one another. First, Lysimachus overthrew Cassander, and then Seleucus killed Lysimachus in battle, leaving

Seleucus in the north and Ptolemy in the south. Thus, the kingdom was divided geographically between the king of the North, and the king of the South. At this point in history, the king of the North and the king of the South were the remains of the Greco-Macedonian Empire.

"Also the king of the South shall become strong, as well as one of his [Alexander's] princes; and he shall gain power over him and have dominion. His dominion shall be a great dominion." Daniel 11:5. When Ptolemy of Egypt (the king of the South) died, his son, Ptolemy Philadelphus, ruled Egypt and Libya. During the 40 years he governed that kingdom, it rose to new heights of grandeur and power. This made it, at one time, superior to other kingdoms.

Seleucus I Nicator (the king of the North) possessed three of the four parts of Alexander's kingdom. Because of the wars against his kingdom, however, he had to call upon Ptolemy for assistance against Demetrius in the Battle of Gaza, in 312 B.C. He subsequently regained the territory he had lost in Mesopotamia. He became the strongest of Alexander's successors, controlling the territory from Hellespont to northern India.

"And at the end of some years they shall join forces, for the daughter of the king of the South shall go to the king of the North to make an agreement." Daniel 11:6. After 35 years of war, Antiochus II Theos (the king of the North), the grandson of Seleucus I Nicator, married Bernice, a daughter of the Egyptian king, Ptolemy II Philadelphus (the king of the South). Antiochus then deposed his former wife Laodice from her position of priority, and deprived her children of succession to the throne.

"But she shall not retain the power of her authority." Daniel 11:6. Bernice subsequently fell out of favor with Antiochus II Theos, and he recalled Laodice, and her children to the court.

"And neither he nor his authority shall stand." Daniel 11:6. Laodice, not willing to take a chance on being deposed again, poisoned Antiochus II Theos, and placed her son, Seleucus Callinicus, in power.

"But she shall be given up, with those who brought her, and with him who begot her, and with him who strengthened her in those times." Daniel 11:6. Through Laodice's influence, Bernice, and her son, and the Egyptian women and attendants in her court, were murdered. This occurred after the death of Bernice's father, Ptolemy II Philadelphus, who doted over Bernice, his favorite daughter.

"But from a branch of her roots one shall arise in his place, who shall

come with an army, enter the fortress of the king of the North, and deal with them and prevail." Daniel 11:7. Ptolemy III, the brother of Bernice, succeeded his father. He ruled Egypt from 246 B.C. to 222 B.C. After forming a large army, he invaded Syria to avenge his sister's death, and killed Laodice.

"And he shall also carry their gods captive to Egypt, with their princes and their precious articles of silver and gold; and he shall continue more years than the king of the North." Daniel 11:8. Ptolemy III (the king of the South) succeeded in his campaign against the kingdom of Seleucus the king of the North. Plundering Syria, he made his way to Babylon, where he found, and returned, the Egyptian gods of silver and gold that Cambyses had taken from Egypt. In recognition, the Egyptian people gave him the name Euergetes (benefactor). As the prophecy stated, he outlived Seleucus Callinicus (the king of the North) by four years.

"Also the king of the North shall come to the kingdom of the king of the South, but shall return to his own land." Daniel 11:9. This verse is a summary of the previous two verses. Ptolemy III (the king of the South) invaded the territory of Seleucus Callinicus (the king of the North), and then returned to his own land of Egypt.

"However his sons shall stir up strife, and assemble a multitude of great forces; and one shall certainly come and overwhelm and pass through; then he shall return to his fortress and stir up strife." Daniel 11:10. Seleucus Callinicus had two sons who set out to regain the territory that had been taken by Ptolemy III Euergetes. The older son succeeded his father, but he was a weak and inefficient leader, and was poisoned by his two generals. His brother, Antiochus Magnus, then became king. He would *"assemble a multitude of great forces"* (Daniel 11:10), and recover Seleucia, and Syria.

"And the king of the South shall be moved with rage, and go out and fight with him, with the king of the North, who shall muster a great multitude; but the multitude shall be given into the hand of his enemy." Daniel 11:11. At that time (222 B.C. to 205 B.C.), the king of Egypt (the king of the South) was Ptolemy IV Philopator, the son of Ptolemy III Euergetes. Ptolemy IV Philopator met Antiochus III the Great, king of Syria (the king of the North), at the battle of Raphia, in 217 B.C. He *"who shall muster a great multitude"* was Antiochus, whose force numbered 70,000 infantry and 5,000 cavalry.

"But the multitude shall be given into the hand of his enemy," i.e., Ptolemy's hand. After a fierce struggle, Antiochus lost 10,000 infantry, 300 cavalry, and 4,000 of his soldiers were taken captive. Defeated, he returned home.

"When he had taken away the multitude, his heart will be lifted up; and he will cast down tens of thousands, but he will not prevail." (Daniel 11:12). Elated by his victory, and full of self-esteem, Ptolemy IV Philopator decided to offer a sacrifice, but was stopped by the priest. Incensed, he made war on the Jews. The historian Eusebius recorded that Ptolemy killed 60,000 Jews in Alexandria.

"For the king of the North will return and muster a multitude greater than the former, and shall certainly come at the end of some years with a great army and much equipment." Daniel 11:13. Fourteen years of peace ensued between Egypt and Syria.

Daniel 11:14–29 — History of Pagan Rome

"Now in those times many shall rise up against the king of the South. Also, violent men of your people shall exalt themselves in fulfillment of the vision, but they shall fall. So the king of the North shall come and build a siege mound, and take a fortified city; and the forces of the South shall not withstand him. Even his choice troops shall have no strength to resist. But he who comes against him shall do according to his own will, and no one shall stand against him. He shall stand in the Glorious Land with destruction in his power.

"He shall also set his face to enter with the strength of his whole kingdom, and upright ones with him; thus shall he do. And he shall give him the daughter of women to destroy it; but she shall not stand with him, or be for him. After this he shall turn his face to the coastlands, and shall take many. But a ruler shall bring the reproach against them to an end; and with the reproach removed, he shall turn back on him. Then he shall turn his face toward the fortress of his own land; but he shall stumble and fall, and not be found.

"There shall arise in his place one who imposes taxes on the glorious kingdom; but within a few days he shall be destroyed, but not in anger or in battle. And in his place shall arise a vile person, to whom they will not give the honor of royalty; but he shall come in peaceably, and seize the kingdom by intrigue. With the force of a flood they shall be swept away from before him and be broken, and also the prince of the covenant. And after the league is made with him he shall act deceitfully, for he shall come up and become strong with a small number of people. He shall enter peaceably, even into the richest places of the province; and he shall do what his fathers have not done, nor his forefathers: he shall disperse among them the plunder, spoil, and riches; and he shall devise his plans against the strongholds, but only for a time.

"He shall stir up his power and his courage against the king of the South with a great army. And the king of the South shall be stirred up to battle with a very great and mighty army; but he shall not stand, for they shall devise plans against him. Yes, those who eat of the portion of his delicacies shall destroy him; his army shall be swept away, and many shall fall down slain. Both these kings' hearts shall be bent on evil, and they shall speak lies at the same table; but it shall not prosper, for the end will still be at the appointed time. While returning to his land with great riches, his heart shall be moved against the holy covenant; so he shall do damage and return to his own land.

"At the appointed time he shall return and go toward the south; but it shall not be like the former or the latter."

Prince of the Covenant

"Now in those times many shall rise up against the king of the South." Daniel 11:14. In chapters 2, 7, and 8, Daniel has presented four kingdoms: Babylon, Medo-Persia, Greece, and Rome. In the angel Gabriel's literal account of these powers, the description of the fourth kingdom begins with verse 14.

In Egypt, Ptolemy IV Philopator (the king of the South) died, and the Ptolemaic dynasty was handed down to his five-year-old son, Ptolemy V Epiphanes. Antiochus III the Great (the king of the North), who was surnamed Megas, saw this as a golden opportunity, and anticipated an easy campaign. By joining forces with Philip V of Macedonia, he expected to easily overthrow the child-king and divide the country, extending both their territories.

"Also, violent men of your people [the original Hebrew states "robberies of the people"] shall exalt themselves in fulfillment of the vision, but they shall fall." Daniel 11:14. Rome had been slowly growing through the years, incorporating one city and town after another. She offered protection, but it came at a price—heavy taxation, and a demand for men to fight in its wars. Wanting to flex her muscles, Rome told Antiochus III to stay out of Egypt and leave the child alone.

"So the king of the North shall come and build a siege mound, and take a fortified city; and the forces of the South shall not withstand him. Even his choice troops shall have no strength to resist" Daniel 11:15. Ignoring the warning given by Rome, Antiochus III turned his attention to the well-fortified city of Gaza, the last town southwest of Palestine, toward Egypt. Gaza held-out against him for a while, but it finally succumbed to the Syrian army. Rome then declared war on Antiochus, and in 168 B.C., at the battle of Pydna, Greece's dominance ended, and Rome became the king of the North.

Three men rose to the leadership of Rome and took over the reins of government. Crassus controlled the treasury, Pompey led the army, and Caesar was the mastermind.

"But he who comes against him shall do according to his own will, and no one shall stand against him." Daniel 11:16. As general of the Roman army, Pompey swept across Asia Minor and Syria, as the Eastern kingdom crumbled before him. *"He shall stand in the Glorious Land with destruction in his power."* Daniel 11:16. In 63 B.C. Pompey entered Palestine following a three-month campaign. The city of Jerusalem fell to Rome, which would control the destiny of Judea for the next two centuries.

"He shall also set his face to enter with the strength of his whole kingdom, and upright ones with him; thus shall he do." Daniel 11:17. When Ptolemy XI (the king of the South) died, he placed his two children, Cleopatra VII and Ptolemy XII, under the guardianship of Rome. Pompey was called to settle a dispute over who was going to rule Egypt, and Cleopatra promptly had Pompey killed as he crossed the Nile river.

Since Rome was the guardian, Julius Caesar stepped-in to fill Pompey's position. *"And he shall give him the daughter of women to destroy it."* Daniel 11:17. Caesar became infatuated with Cleopatra, so he espoused her cause and made her his mistress. However, this was short-lived: *"but she shall not stand with him, or be for him."* Daniel 11:17. Cleopatra turned her affection to Mark Antony, Caesar's enemy, and exerted her influence against Rome.

"After this he shall turn his face to the coastlands, and shall take many."

Daniel 11:18. Caesar left Egypt, and made his way down the northern coast of Africa. Cities and islands in his path submitted to him, and he returned to Rome in triumph, remaining its dictator for the rest of his life.

"But a ruler shall bring the reproach against them to an end; and with the reproach removed, he shall turn back on him." Daniel 11:18. Brutus, a close friend of Caesar's, turned his back on him, leading a movement to eliminate his dictatorship.

"Then he shall turn his face toward the fortress of his own land; but he shall stumble and fall, and not be found." Daniel 11:19. Everything seemed favorable on the Ides, or fifteenth day of March, as Julius Caesar shared great plans for Rome in the presence of the senate. At a given signal, his enemies grabbed their concealed weapons and stabbed him 23 times. He stumbled and fell at the base of the statue of Pompey. Mark Antony should have succeeded Caesar but he had run-off with Cleopatra, both of whom later committed suicide. Caesar left no legitimate heirs, but his nephew Octavius (Augustus), who had been appointed his heir, succeeded him.

"There shall arise in his place one who imposes taxes on the glorious kingdom; but within a few days he shall be destroyed, but not in anger or in battle." Daniel 11:20. This taxation on the glorious land is recorded in the New Testament: *"And it came to pass in those days that a decree went out from Caesar Augustus that all the world should be registered [The King James Version states 'taxed']."* Luke 2:1. Augustus' taxes were light because they were universal. The inclusion of Israel in his decree is what brought Joseph and Mary to Bethlehem. Caesar Augustus ruled for 40 years, and he firmly established the Roman Empire. He died peacefully in his own bed.

"And in his place shall arise a vile person, to whom they will not give the honor of royalty; but he shall come in peaceably, and seize the kingdom by intrigue." Daniel 11:21. Augustus had no son of his own; but his wife, Livia, urged him to appoint Tiberius, her son by a previous marriage, as his successor. He refused, saying Tiberius was too vile to follow him as emperor. Instead, Augustus appointed Agrippa to succeed him, but Agrippa died before he could do so. Through the urging of his wife, Augustus finally relented and appointed Tiberius—a man so vile that the residents of the city of Rome rejoiced when he died.

"With the force of a flood they shall be swept away from before him

and be broken, and also the prince of the covenant." Daniel 11:22. It was during the reign of Tiberius that Christ (the Prince of the covenant) was crucified, just as had been prophesied: "*Then He shall confirm a covenant with many for one week; but in the middle of the week He shall bring an end to sacrifice and offering.*" Daniel 9:27. Up to this point, we have seen the kings of the North and South change from one literal king to another. However, from Daniel 11:22 on, the texts center more on the king of the North being Rome, and the king of the South being those who stood in opposition to Rome. Verses 23 through 29 are a summary of the exploits of Pagan Rome. Note that the identity of the kings does not change.

"*And after the league is made with him he shall act deceitfully, for he shall come up and become strong with a small number of people.*" Daniel 11:23. Pagan Rome began in Italy with "*a small number of people.*"

"*He shall enter peaceably, even into the richest places of the province; and he shall do what his fathers have not done, nor his forefathers.*" Daniel 11:24. Up until this time, nations gained new territory by force; however, by promising friendship and protection to everyone who appealed to it, Rome became a type of referee. This was a new idea. Rome posed as a defender of the weak, and this was one of the primary ways it succeeded in so-broadly expanding its kingdom.

"*He shall disperse among them the plunder, spoil, and riches; and he shall devise his plans against the strongholds, but only for a time.*" Daniel 11:24. Rome shared the spoils from its conquests with those who came under its protection. As Pagan Rome's strength increased, it sent out armies against those who stood in its way. One of its first major conquests was Carthage, an ancient city in Northern Africa, in 146 B.C.. Rome's victory over Carthage changed the course of history, for the ancient civilization of the Mediterranean would now pass to the modern world via Southern Europe, instead of Northern Africa. Next, Pagan Rome brought Syria under its control, followed by Asia Minor, and Palestine.

"*He shall stir up his power and his courage against the king of the South with a great army. And the king of the South shall be stirred up to battle with a very great and mighty army; but he shall not stand, for they shall devise plans against him.*" Daniel 11:25. As Rome extended its territory, it decided to conquer Egypt (the king of the South). This prophecy was fulfilled in the conflict between Augustus (the king of the North) and Mark Antony (the king of the South). Outwardly, these two brothers-in-law were in alliance with one another. *"Yes, those who eat of the portion of his delicacies shall destroy him; his army shall be swept away, and many shall fall down slain. Both these kings' hearts shall be bent on evil, and they shall speak lies at the same table; but it shall not prosper, for the end will still be at the appointed time."* Daniel 11:26, 27. Augustus defeated Mark Antony at the battle of Actium, in 31 B.C. Mark Antony's allies, disgusted over his infatuation with Cleopatra, deserted him and joined Augustus. Mark Antony subsequently committed suicide.

"While returning to his land with great riches." Daniel 11:28. Augustus triumphantly returned from Egypt with great riches.

"His heart shall be moved against the holy covenant; so he shall do damage and return to his own land." Daniel 11:28. In 70 A.D., Rome sent an army under Titus to put down a revolt in Jerusalem, burning the temple to the ground, and destroying the city.

The Pagan Roman Empire made the roads and waterways safe, extending travel to many parts of the world, and making it possible for the gospel to spread rapidly. Roman soldiers marched down the roads carrying signs which stated, *"Pax Romana"* (Roman Peace). By the second century, however, Rome was growing old, and changes were taking place.

"At the appointed time he shall return and go toward the south; but it shall not be like the former or the latter." Daniel 11:29. Constantine moved the capital of the empire from Rome to Constantinople, and Rome lost its prestige. The barbarian hordes from the north began to attack, and the Pagan Roman Empire was broken apart.

Daniel 11:30–39 — History of Papal Rome

"For ships from Cyprus shall come against him; therefore he shall be grieved, and return in rage against the holy covenant, and do damage.

"So he shall return and show regard for those who forsake the holy covenant. And forces shall be mustered by him, and they shall defile the sanctuary fortress; then they shall take away the daily sacrifices, and place there the abomination of desolation. Those who do wickedly against the covenant he shall corrupt with flattery; but the people who know their God shall be strong, and carry out great exploits. And those of the people who understand shall instruct many; yet for many days they shall fall by sword and flame, by captivity and plundering. Now when they fall, they

shall be aided with a little help; but many shall join with them by intrigue. And some of those of understanding shall fall, to refine them, purify them, and make them white, until the time of the end; because it is still for the appointed time.

"Then the king shall do according to his own will: he shall exalt and magnify himself above every god, shall speak blasphemies against the God of gods, and shall prosper till the wrath has been accomplished; for what has been determined shall be done. He shall regard neither the God of his fathers nor the desire of women, nor regard any god; for he shall exalt himself above them all. But in their place he shall honor a god of fortresses; and a god which his fathers did not know he shall honor with gold and silver, with precious stones and pleasant things. Thus he shall act against the strongest fortresses with a foreign god, which he shall acknowledge, and advance its glory; and he shall cause them to rule over many, and divide the land for gain."

Key to Prophecy — Papal Supremacy

"For ships from Cyprus shall come against him." Daniel 11:30. The Vandals, one of the ten Germanic tribes, sailed their ships into the Roman fleet and set it on fire. This destroyed almost the entire Roman navy, and hastened the demise of the empire. Rome was certainly grieved, just as the text indicates: *"he shall be grieved."* Daniel 11:30. Due to the unspeakable deeds perpetrated against Rome by this barbarian tribe, even to this day, those involved in malicious destruction are called "vandals," and their acts are referred to as "vandalism."

"And return in rage against the holy covenant, and do damage." Daniel 11:30. The Germanic tribes of the north were tearing the Roman Empire apart, and the emperor, Justinian, was losing control. Due to the growth of Christianity, the empire was half Christian, and the only thing that seemed to be holding it together was the church. Despite the fact that the capital had been moved to Constantinople, the people still looked to Rome for guidance and leadership. So they turned to the bishop of Rome for direction. Taking the scepter in his hand, he took over the seat of Caesar, becoming not only the spiritual head, but also the political head of the empire. This united church and state.

A church has no power of its own, but given civil power, it can enforce its dogmas via civil laws and military might—even if its dogmas are against the Scripture. Just as the little horn (Papal Rome) rose out of the fourth beast (Pagan Rome) in Daniel 7, so now, in Daniel 11:30, the Roman Empire begins the transition from Pagan, to Papal Rome.

"And forces shall be mustered by him, and they shall defile the sanctuary fortress; then they shall take away the daily sacrifices, and place there the abomination of desolation." Daniel 11:31. Verses 31–35 place the Papal Power in control. With its last serious opposition eliminated (the Ostrogoths, in 538 A.D.), the Papacy showed her crushing power: *"and force shall be mustered by him"* (Daniel 11:31). With the Papal Power now in control of the empire, and the arms of state at its command, persecution followed.

The phrase *"daily sacrifice"* is used in Daniel 8:11–13; 11:31; and 12:11; and the phrases *"daily sacrifice"* and *"abomination of desolation"* are used together in Daniel 11:31 and 12:11. In each case, the Scripture is referring to what Rome would do. When Jesus explained the signs of His return, He counseled His believers to watch for the *"abomination of desolation"*: *"Therefore when you see the 'abomination of desolation,' spoken of by Daniel the prophet, standing in the holy place ..."* (Matthew 24:15).

Daniel 8:12 makes this statement regarding the Horn as Pagan, and then Papal, Rome, *"Because of transgression, an army was given over to the horn to oppose the daily sacrifices; and he cast truth down to the ground. He did all this and prospered."* This refers to when the Roman army, under Titus, invaded Jerusalem, destroying the temple and burning the city to the ground, in 70 A.D. As the Roman soldiers entered the city, they pitched standards of their pagan gods as a sign of victory. This sign of idolatry was an *"abomination"* to the Jews, and it led to the *"desolation"* of the temple.

Just before Jesus was crucified, He told the Jewish leaders, *"See! Your house is left unto you desolate"* (Matthew 23:38). Just so, as Jesus hung on the cross, the veil in the temple was miraculously torn from top to bottom, showing that the sacrifices and offerings had come to an end, because He to whom they pointed had given His life for the world.

In Daniel 11:31, the angel Gabriel takes us from the collapse of Pagan Rome to the rise of Papal Rome. The word "sacrifice" is not in the original Hebrew text, but it is implied because the Hebrew word for daily is *tamid*, which means "regularly." The sacrifice was offered daily in the temple as part of the Jewish worship service.

The ministry of Christ in Heaven as our High Priest (see Hebrews 8:1–2) is one of the great truths that she (Papal Rome) cast to the ground. Just as the sacrifice was offered daily in the temple (or regularly, as the Hebrew word *tamid* implies), so Christ now ministers regularly in our behalf in the sanctuary in heaven. Jesus' ministry as our Mediator in heaven will continue until sin is no more, and He has set up His Kingdom which will never end. There is something else that was done on a regular basis, and which will continue throughout eternity, *"And it shall come to pass that from one New Moon to another, and from one Sabbath to another, all flesh shall come to worship before Me, says the Lord."* (Isaiah 66:23), i.e., a day the Christian church was instructed to keep regularly, as part of its worship. The one thing God instructs Christians to do regularly is to *"Remember the Sabbath day, to keep it holy. Six days you shall labor and do all your work, <u>but the seventh day is the Sabbath of the Lord your God.</u> In it you shall do no work: you, nor your son, nor your daughter, nor your male servant, nor your female servant, nor your cattle, nor your stranger who is within your gates. For in six days the LORD made the heavens and the earth, the sea, and all that is in them, and rested the seventh day. Therefore the LORD blessed the Sabbath day and hallowed it."* **Emphasis provided.** Exodus 20:8–11.

One of the first actions of Papal Rome was to take away the daily sacrifice and set up "the abomination of desolation." In 538 A.D., Rome made a law doing away with the Sabbath, and setting up "the abomination of desolation." It reads: "Whereas the people are persuaded that they ought not to travel on the Lord's day with the horses, or oxen and carriages, or to prepare anything for food, or to do anything conducive to the cleanliness of houses or men, things which belong to Jewish rather than Christian observances; we have ordained that on the Lord's day what was before lawful to be done may still be done. But from rural work, i.e., plowing, cultivating vines, reaping, mowing, thrashing, clearing away thorns or hedging, we judge it better to abstain, that the people may the more readily come to the churches and have leisure for prayers. <u>If any one be found doing the works forbidden above, let him be punished, not as the civil authorities may direct, but as the ecclesiastical powers may determine.</u>" (Emphasis supplied). (Council of Orleans III, can. xxviii; Binius, tome xi, p. 496; or Labbe, ix, p. 19. *A Critical History of Sunday Legislation from 321 to 1888 A.D.*, 64.)

The significance of this law was that it forbade work on Sunday, and that the church—rather than the civil authority—would carry out the punishment. This confirmed that church and state had come together in the Roman Empire, placing the Papal Power in control. She had replaced the Lord's seventh day Sabbath with the first day of the week, a day named after the sun god.

Again, Papal Rome took away the "daily," i.e., the time God set aside for Christians to worship regularly, each week, on His seventh day Sabbath. In addition, she changed the day of worship to Sunday—a day dedicated to the sun god by pagan sun-worshippers, which the Scripture considers an abomination (See Ezekiel 8:16–17). Daniel 12 gives additional information concerning the *"daily sacrifice"* and *"the abomination of desolation."*

"Those who do wickedly against the covenant he shall corrupt with flattery; but the people who know their God shall be strong, and carry out great exploits. And those of the people who understand shall instruct many; yet for many days they shall fall by sword and flame, by captivity and plundering. Now when they fall, they shall be aided with a little help; but many shall join with them by intrigue." Daniel 11:32–33. These verses describe the time of Papal supremacy. With the rise of Papal power, the world moved into a time known as The Dark Ages (approximately 476 A.D. to 1000 A.D.).

During the Dark Ages, superstition and tradition ruled the day. The church was the final authority on everything, and the common people were considered little more than animals. Few people could read or write; Bibles were chained to church and monastery walls, and the common people were told that they were too ignorant to understand it.

Some fought against these conditions: *"But the people who know their God shall be strong, and carry out great exploits. And those of the people who understand shall instruct many."* Daniel 11:32–33. The Word of God was shared through the work of people like the Waldenses, Albigenses, Hussites, and Lollards.

"Yet for many days they shall fall by sword and flame, by captivity and plundering. Now when they fall, they shall be aided with a little help;" Daniel 11:33–34. Men like Huss, Jerome, Knox and thousands of others were martyred for their faith.

"And some of those of understanding shall fall, to refine them, purify

them, and make them white, until the time of the end; because it is still for the appointed time." Daniel 11:35. Beginning with her assumption of power in 538 A.D., and continuing for over a thousand years, Papal Rome persecuted those who did not accept her teachings, as the Bible states, "*Knowing that tribulation produces perseverance.*" Romans 5:3. Through trials and tribulations, our characters are perfected, and made white by faith in the righteousness of our Lord and Savior.

The book of Daniel mentions the phrase, "*The time of the end,*" five times (see Daniel 8:17; 11:35, 40; 12:4, 9). All these verses refer to the same period. In Daniel 7:25, God gave Papal Rome a set period of time: "*Then the saints shall be given into his hand for a time and times and half a time.*"

At the end of 1,260 years, "*the appointed time*" had come for the beginning of "the time of the end." In 1798 A.D., Napoleon's general, Louis-Alexandre Berthier, marched into Rome and took Pope Pius VI prisoner, ending the rule of Papal Rome. The "time of the end" is the period from 1798 A.D. until the Second Coming of Jesus; in other words, we are living in "the time of the end."

"*Then the king shall do according to his own will: he shall exalt and magnify himself above every god, shall speak blasphemies against the God of gods, and shall prosper till the wrath has been accomplished; for what has been determined shall be done. He shall regard neither the God of his fathers nor the desire of women, nor regard any god; for he shall exalt himself above them all. But in their place he shall honor a god of fortresses; and a god which his fathers did not know he shall honor with gold and silver, with precious stones and pleasant things. Thus he shall act against the strongest fortresses with a foreign god, which he shall acknowledge, and advance its glory; and he shall cause them to rule over many, and divide the land for gain.*" Daniel 11:36–39.

Beginning with verse 30, Gabriel has been talking about one power— Papal Rome. The church gained ever-more civil power worldwide, and with it came pride, riches, and conceit. Verses 36 through 39 relate to the condition of the church. During the 1,260 years, the Papal church was primarily interested in exalting itself, and in gaining more control, issuing statements such as this: "*We [the popes] hold upon this earth the place of God Almighty.*" (The Great Encyclical Letter of Pope Leo the XIII (New York: Benziger, 1903) p. 304).

"He shall regard neither the God of his fathers nor the desire of women."
Daniel 11:37. Contrary to Scripture (Matthew 19:11–12), the Papacy
demanded that priests practice celibacy.

"He shall honor with gold and silver, with precious stones and pleasant
things." Daniel 11:38.

The church funded the building of St. Peter's Cathedral with indulgences
sold to the poor.

"[The king] shall prosper till the wrath has been accomplished; for what
has been determined shall be done." Daniel 11:36. At the end of the 18th
century, the church owned large portions of land called the Papal States,
and the coffers of the church were full. God "determined" when the
Papacy would end. The prophecy was fulfilled in 1798 A.D., right on
time.

Daniel 11:40-45 — Papal Rome Reestablished

"At the time of the end the king of the South shall attack him; and the
king of the North shall come against him like a whirlwind, with chariots,
horsemen, and with many ships; and he shall enter the countries, overwhelm
them, and pass through. He shall also enter the Glorious Land, and many
countries shall be overthrown; but these shall escape from his hand: Edom,
Moab, and the prominent people of Ammon. He shall stretch out his hand
against the countries, and the land of Egypt shall not escape. He shall have
power over the treasures of gold and silver, and over all the precious things
of Egypt; also the Libyans and Ethiopians shall follow at his heels. But news
from the east and the north shall trouble him; therefore he shall go out with
great fury to destroy and annihilate many. And he shall plant the tents of
his palace between the seas and the glorious holy mountain; yet he shall
come to his end, and no one will help him."

Yet He Shall Come to His End

Key to Prophecy

Verse 40 states, "At the time of the end," indicating that the
remainder of chapter 11 concerns the time just before Jesus
comes again. I wish I could speak with as much certainty about future
events as I do about those that have taken place in the past, but this is
one of the frailties of man. We are unable to see the future.

However, one of the marvelous things about prophecy is that it gives us
a glimpse of things that are going to take place. From our study of Daniel,

we have learned that only four kingdoms are described in chapters 2, 7, and 8, i.e., Babylon, Medo-Persia, Greece, and Pagan, and Papal Rome. These kingdoms encompassed the period of time from Daniel's day until the Second Coming of Christ. Therefore, in keeping with what the angel Gabriel has revealed to Daniel, we should not expect a different power to arise than what has been revealed.

"The king of the North" is the same power as the beast in Revelation that received a deadly wound, and its deadly wound was healed. When Napoleon's general, Berthier, took the Pope prisoner in 1798, that power received the "deadly wound" spoken of in Revelation 13:3. All of its power and wealth was stripped away, and for one hundred years, it had to function like any other church, i.e., without civil power. In 1929, Italy's Benito Mussolini signed the Lateran Treaty with the Vatican, re-establishing the Papacy, returning civil power to it, and creating an independent Vatican state/nation. Therefore, to be consistent with the other chapters of Daniel, Rome must be *"The king of the North,"* the fourth kingdom. Rome, in the form of the Roman Catholic Church, assumed civil power. She, with her partners—the false prophet and the dragon discussed in Revelation 16:13—will become the leading political and religious leaders on earth.

"He shall enter the countries, overwhelm them, and pass through." Daniel 11:40. This will not necessarily be accomplished by arms, since the Papal church is more interested in making the people members, either by birth, coercion, or acceptance. Her membership has grown to over 1.2 billion members in the past 80 years.

"He shall also enter the Glorious Land, and many countries shall be overthrown; but these shall escape from his hand: Edom, Moab, and the prominent people of Ammon. He shall stretch out his hand against the countries, and the land of Egypt shall not escape. He shall have power over the treasures of gold and silver, and over all the precious things of Egypt; also the Libyans and Ethiopians shall follow at his heels." Daniel 11:41–43. These verses parallel Revelation 17, with the woman (Babylon) sitting on the scarlet–colored beast that the entire world, including the Glorious Land (the Middle East), will follow. In my opinion, the words of Gabriel seem to indicate that there may be a confrontation between Catholicism and Islam. The countries listed are Islamic in belief, and from what the Scripture implies, the descendents of *"Edom, Moab, and the prominent*

people of Ammon" which make up modern day Jordan, will not go along with the Papacy, but Egypt, Libya, and Ethiopia will follow in the footsteps of Catholicism. Only time will tell how this will all work out. Jesus said, *"And now I have told you before it comes, that when it does come to pass, you may believe."* John 14:29.

"But news from the east and the north shall trouble him; therefore he shall go out with great fury to destroy and annihilate many. And he shall plant the tents of his palace between the seas and the glorious holy mountain; yet he shall come to his end, and no one will help him." Daniel 11:44–45. News coming from the east and north is troublesome, because it means there is internal strife there. The same events are pictured in Revelation 17, when the ten kings turn on the woman (spiritual Babylon), and kill her. The king of the North and Babylon are the same entity. Many of the nations that turn, and follow the Papacy in setting up its kingdom, will finally turn against her. The Papal Empire will begin to crumble, *"He shall come to his end, and no one will help him."* Daniel 11:45.

Gabriel has given a detailed account of many of the prominent nations of the earth, from Daniel's time until the Second Coming of Christ. However, utmost in Daniel's mind is the location and condition of God's people. Chapter 12 reveals the marvelous deliverance of the followers of Christ in the very last days.

DANIEL 12

1 "At that time Michael shall stand up, The great prince who stands watch over the sons of your people; And there shall be a time of trouble, Such as never was since there was a nation, Even to that time.
And at that time your people shall be delivered, Every one who is found written in the book.
2 And many of those who sleep in the dust of the earth shall awake, Some to everlasting life, Some to shame and everlasting contempt.
3 Those who are wise shall shine Like the brightness of the firmament, And those who turn many to righteousness Like the stars forever and ever.
4 "But you, Daniel, shut up the words, and seal the book until the time of the end; many shall run to and fro, and knowledge shall increase."
5 Then I, Daniel, looked; and there stood two others, one on this riverbank and the other on that riverbank.
6 And one said to the man clothed in linen, who was above the waters of the river, "How long shall the fulfillment of these wonders be?"
7 Then I heard the man clothed in linen, who was above the waters of the river, when he held up his right hand and his left hand to heaven, and swore by Him who lives forever, that it shall be for a time, times, and half a time; and when the power of the holy people has been completely shattered, all these things shall be finished.
8 Although I heard, I did not understand. Then I said, "My lord, what shall be the end of these things?"
9 And he said, "Go your way, Daniel, for the words are closed up and sealed till the time of the end.
10 Many shall be purified, made white, and refined, but the wicked shall do wickedly; and none of the wicked shall understand, but the wise shall understand.
11 "And from the time that the daily sacrifice is taken away, and the abomination of desolation is set up, there shall be one thousand two hundred and ninety days.
12 Blessed is he who waits, and comes to the one thousand three hundred and thirty-five days.
13 "But you, go your way till the end; for you shall rest, and will arise to your inheritance at the end of the days."

CHAPTER 12

The Five Wonders

Inside this Chapter

Daniel 12:1–3 — The Five Wonders

"At that time Michael shall stand up,
The great prince who stands watch over the sons of your people;
And there shall be a time of trouble,
Such as never was since there was a nation,
Even to that time.
And at that time your people shall be delivered,
Every one who is found written in the book.
And many of those who sleep in the dust of the earth shall awake,
Some to everlasting life,
Some to shame and everlasting contempt.
Those who are wise shall shine
Like the brightness of the firmament,
And those who turn many to righteousness
Like the stars forever and ever."

Bible Chapters

The Geneva Bible was the first English Bible printed with chapters and verses. The punctuation in the Bible, including its division into chapters and verses, is not inspired; it was added centuries after the books of the Bible were written, by people who, although well-intentioned, were not inspired.

As happens in any large human endeavor, many mistakes were made. For example, the first three verses of Daniel 12 should be the last three verses of chapter 11. The last verse of Daniel 11 describes the end of the *"king of the North"* by stating: *"Yet he shall come to his end, and no one will help him."* Daniel 11:45. Daniel 12:1 then opens (with *"At that time …,"* i.e., at the time of the end of the *"king of the North."*

Most of this chapter concerns future events, and the only sure foundation for future events is what Scripture reveals about the time of the end. The angel Gabriel begins this chapter by telling the end of the story, so that Daniel would know what the end of God's people would be.

After much study and prayer, the following remarks are my understanding of what Gabriel explained to Daniel.

The Wonders

First Wonder: *Michael Stands Up*

"At that time Michael shall stand up, the great Prince who stands watch over the sons of your people." Daniel 12:1.

We read about Michael in chapter 10, so please return to that chapter and re-read the explanation of Daniel 10:13. One of the attributes of Michael is that He is our Mediator or High Priest in the Sanctuary in Heaven (see Hebrews 7:25). When His mediation ends, He will stand up and say, *"It is done!"* Revelation 16:17. Probation will then close for the human race, after which there will be no possibility for any person to change or repent (see Revelation 22:11).

Second Wonder: *Time of Trouble*

"And there shall be a time of trouble, such as never was since there was a nation, even to that time." Daniel 12:1.

As probation closes, the time of trouble, and the pouring out of the seven last plagues, will begin: *"The temple was filled with smoke from the glory of God and from His power, and no one was able to enter the temple till the seven plagues of the seven angels were completed. Then I heard a loud voice from the temple saying to the seven angels, 'Go and pour out the bowls of the wrath of God on the earth.'"* Revelation 15:8; 16:1. The plagues are a part of the punishment of the wicked, representing the wrath of God upon those who have chosen to oppose, rather than follow, the Lord. They will not fall on the righteous, *"No evil shall befall you, nor shall any plague come near your dwelling; for He shall give His angels charge over you, to keep you in all your ways."* Psalm 91:10–11.

When the Beast of Revelation 13 joins with the False Prophet and the Dragon (see Revelation 16:13–14), they will form what the Scripture refers to as "Babylon." This tri-fold union will unite the world in passing a universal law, stating that everyone must have a "mark" in order to buy or sell. The "mark" issue will involve "worship," either to the beast or to God. **For more on this subject, please read this volume's companion book "Revelation, Pure and Simple."**

Revelation 14:12 tells us that those who keep the commandments of God will not receive the Mark of the Beast. The Papacy, i.e., the *"beast rising up out of the sea"* in Revelation 13:1, states that the mark of her authority is her changing of God's Sabbath: "Protestants . . . accept Sunday rather than Saturday as the day for public worship after the Catholic Church made the change. . . . But the Protestant mind does not seem to realize that . . . in observing Sunday, they are accepting the authority of the spokesman for the church, the Pope." (*Our Sunday Visitor*, February 15, 1950.)

According to the Bible, the penalty for not accepting the Mark of the Beast, i.e., the Beast's *"mark,"* will be death (see Revelation 13:15). This is why it will be a time of trouble for the followers of Christ.

Jesus said, *"If you love Me, keep My commandments."* John 14:15. The followers of the Lord have learned to walk by faith, and during this time of trouble, they will be sustained by the power of God. Those who haven't already suffered martyrdom for refusing to accept the Beast's mark will be protected by holy angels once the seven last plagues begin to fall. The plagues that fall upon all who accept the Beast's mark will be terrible. The plagues cannot last long, or the whole world would be destroyed. This will take place just before the Lord returns.

Third Wonder: *God's People Delivered*

"And at that time your people shall be delivered, every one who is found written in the book." Daniel 12:1.

From the world's point of view, it will look as if all who have refused to accept the Mark of the Beast will be killed. All earthly support will be removed from them. Each person who keeps the commandments of God, including following Christ in keeping His fourth commandment (the seventh-day Sabbath), will be in this situation.

The day and hour of their execution will be announced, but the promises of God are sure, and will not fail. *"And shall God not avenge His own elect who cry out day and night to Him, though He bears long with them? I tell you that He will avenge them speedily."* Luke 18:7–8.

Daniel 12:12 promises a special blessing to those who wait patiently upon the Lord, and as surely as He delivered the children of Israel from Pharaoh and his army, He will miraculously deliver His people from being afflicted by the plagues. More detail will be given when we get to verse 12.

Fourth Wonder: *Special Resurrection*

The Bible tells about two major resurrections of the dead; the resurrection of life, and the resurrection of condemnation: *"Do not marvel at this; for the hour is coming in which all who are in the graves will hear His voice and come forth — those who have done good, to the resurrection of life, and those who have done evil, to the resurrection of condemnation"* John 5:28–29. In 1 Thessalonians 4:16, Paul speaks of the resurrection of life as the first resurrection: *"For the Lord Himself will descend from heaven with a shout, with the voice of an archangel, and with the trumpet of God. And the dead in Christ will rise first."*

Revelation 20:6 explains these two resurrections further: *"Blessed and holy is he who has part in the first resurrection. Over such the second death has no power, but they shall be priests of God and of Christ, and shall reign with Him a thousand years."*

Revelation 20:5 states: *"But the rest of the dead did not live again until the thousand years were finished."* This verse has to refer to the lost, because those who died in Christ came forth in the first resurrection. One thousand years separate these two major resurrections.

"And many of those who sleep in the dust of the earth shall awake, some to everlasting life, some to shame and everlasting contempt." Daniel 12:2. This text in Daniel is not speaking of either of the two major resurrections; instead, it refers to another, special resurrection that will occur just prior to Jesus' Second Coming. Revelation 1:7 mentions it as well: *"Behold, He is coming with clouds, and every eye will see Him, even they who pierced Him. And all the tribes of the earth will mourn because of Him. Even so, Amen."* Those who were foremost in the crucifixion of Christ will be resurrected to see Him coming in the clouds of heaven. This will occur prior to the first resurrection, and 1,000 years before the resurrection of the wicked. Jesus spoke specifically of this special resurrection when talking to Caiaphas, the High Priest at the time of His trial. Jesus said to him, *"It is as you said. Nevertheless, I say to you, hereafter you will see the Son of Man sitting at the right hand of the Power, and coming on the clouds of heaven."* Matthew 26:64. Here, Jesus addressed Caiaphas personally, telling him that he would see Him as He returns.

A similar, special resurrection occurred at the time of Jesus' death. *"Then, behold, the veil of the temple was torn in two from top to bottom; and the earth quaked, and the rocks were split, and the graves were opened; and many bodies of the saints who had fallen asleep were raised; and coming out of the graves after His resurrection, they went into the holy city and appeared to many."* Matthew 27:51–53.

The major participants in the crucifixion of Christ, and those who have persecuted His people, will come forth from the grave to see Him returning to redeem His people. Daniel 12:2 also mentions another group in this special resurrection, who will rise *"to everlasting life."* They are those who will suffer persecution and martyrdom during the time of the end, before the plagues begin.

Fifth Wonder: *Shine Like the Stars*

"Those who are wise shall shine like the brightness of the firmament, and those who turn many to righteousness like the stars forever and ever." Daniel 12:3.

Many Scriptures mention shining in God's kingdom: *"Then the righteous will shine forth as the sun in the kingdom of their Father. He who has ears to hear, let him hear!"* Matthew 13:43. The experience of Moses on Mount Sinai gives insight into this glory of God; and how to shine like a star: *"And he said, 'Please, show me Your glory.' And the Lord said, 'Here is a place by Me, and you shall stand on the rock. So it shall be, while My glory passes by, that I will put you in the cleft of the rock, and will cover you with My hand while I pass by. Then I will take away My hand, and you shall see My back; but My face shall not be seen'. Now the Lord descended in the cloud and stood with him there, and proclaimed the name of the Lord. And the Lord passed before him and proclaimed, 'The Lord, the Lord God, merciful and gracious, longsuffering, and abounding in goodness and truth, keeping mercy for thousands, forgiving iniquity and transgression and sin.'"* Exodus 33:18, 21–23; 34:5–7. What Moses saw was the character of God. This is His glory. Because of this experience, Moses' face shone so brightly that he had to veil it, except when he went in before the Lord.

There must be a work of transformation in the lives of God's people. We are to become like our Lord: *"But we all, with unveiled face, beholding as in a mirror the glory of the Lord, are being transformed into the same image from glory to glory, just as by the Spirit of the Lord."* 2 Corinthians 3:18. Our characters must shine as a witness of God's grace and mercy, *"That you may become blameless and harmless, children of God without fault in the midst of a crooked and perverse generation, among whom you shine as lights in the world."* Philippians 2:15. This takes place by a daily surrender to the work of the Holy Spirit in our lives. Only He can perform this task, which the Bible refers to as *"sanctification"* (see 2 Thessalonians

2:13–14.) It may be painful, but it brings great blessings: *"But the fruit of the Spirit is love, joy, peace, longsuffering, kindness, goodness, faithfulness, gentleness, self-control. Against such there is no law."* Galatians 5:22–23.

If we want Jesus to return, that is what He is waiting for. His grace changes a sinner into a child of God. This change must be evident in the lives of His people today: *"Let your light so shine before men, that they may see your good works and glorify your Father in heaven."* Matthew 5:16.

Daniel 12:4 — Time of the End

"But you, Daniel, shut up the words, and seal the book until the time of the end; many shall run to and fro, and knowledge shall increase."

Seal the Book

Consider This The phrase *"time of the end"* appears five times in the book of Daniel (Daniel 8:17; 11:35, 40; 12:4, 9). The Hebrew wording is identical in each case, showing that it refers to the same time period. Both the fourth and ninth verses of Daniel 12 use the expression *"time of the end,"* but for clarification, the translators inserted the words *"even,"* or *"until,"* pointing to a specific time when the prophecy would no longer be *"sealed,"* and the time of the end would begin. Not until we reached the *"time of the end"* could the prophecies concerning the end of time be understood, and preached. Even though Daniel didn't understand the prophecies, he was told that in the last days knowledge would be increased, referring to man's understanding of this prophecy. The term *"time of the end"* is used again in verse 9, where it will be looked at in greater detail.

Daniel 12:5–6 — Two Angels and Christ

"Then I, Daniel, looked; and there stood two others, one on this riverbank and the other on that riverbank. And one said to the man clothed in linen, who was above the waters of the river, 'How long shall the fulfillment of these wonders be?'"

Fulfillment of the Wonders

Consider This Two heavenly beings are having a conversation with the Man above the river concerning the five wonders. This is the same Man as the *"Man clothed in linen"* who talked to Daniel in chapter 10, and who gave the aged prophet comfort and assurance regarding the closing events of this earth's history.

In their discussion about the wonders, the two angels ask, *"How long shall the fulfillment of these wonders be?"* In our study of the five wonders in the first three verses, we learned the following:

First, both the Hebrew and English versions imply that they are still in the future.

Secondly, they take place after probation closes for humanity.

Thirdly, they happen just before Jesus returns.

The answer to the question asked in Daniel 12:6 comes in the next three verses.

Daniel 12:7–9 — Time, Times, and Half a Time

"Then I heard the man clothed in linen, who was above the waters of the river, when he held up his right hand and his left hand to heaven, and swore by Him who lives forever, that it shall be for a time, times, and half a time; and when the power of the holy people has been completely shattered, all these things shall be finished. Although I heard, I did not understand. Then I said, 'My lord, what shall be the end of these things?' And he said, 'Go your way, Daniel, for the words are closed up and sealed till the time of the end.'"

1,260 Days

Key to Prophecy

The terminology *"time, times, and half a time"* is not new to us in our study of Daniel. It appears in Daniel 7:25, Daniel 12:7, and Revelation 12:14. In all three cases, the words in both Hebrew and Greek mean a period of time. Please return to chapter 7:25 and re-read the explanation for this term. The Bible uses this time prophecy more than any other.

When speaking about God's people in Revelation 11:3 and 12:6, it is referred to as the exact number of 1,260. In reference to the wicked, Revelation 11:2 and 13:5 refer to it as 42 months. The *"time and times and half a time"* of Daniel 7:25 and 12:7 refers to the time of persecution. All cases refer to the time of Papal Supremacy, beginning in 538 A.D., when the Catholic Church began to enforce civil power, and continuing until Napoleon's general, Berthier, took Pope Pius VI prisoner in 1798 A.D., ending the time of Papal rule. Daniel was told the prophecy will be *"closed up and sealed till the time of the end,"* which began in 1798 A.D. Thus, the Man clothed in linen gives the period in which *"all these things shall be finished."*

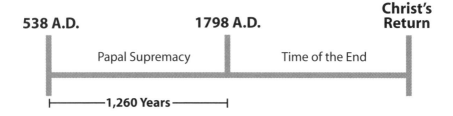

Daniel 12:10 —The Wise Shall Understand

"Many shall be purified, made white, and refined, but the wicked shall do wickedly; and none of the wicked shall understand, but the wise shall understand."

The Former Rain and The Latter Rain

There are many references to the former and latter rain in Scripture. In the literal sense, the "former rain" (early rain, or first rain) occurred in the autumn of the year, at the planting of the winter crops. This rain was required for the seed to sprout and get a good start before winter set in.

Figuratively, the "former rain" is also used to describe the outpouring of the Holy Spirit on the Day of Pentecost, which fulfilled the first part of the prophecy found in Joel 2:23, and which is referenced by Peter in Acts 2. The Holy Spirit was poured out like rain on the Day of Pentecost.

The Holy Spirit is given to carry God's church through spiritual growth, in preparation for the "latter rain." Literally, the "latter rain" came in the spring, at the end of the rainy season. It was needed for the grain to finish maturing before the harvest. Please note that, without the "former rain," the "latter rain" was of no value.

The figurative reference to the "latter rain" fulfills the second half of the prophecy found in Joel 2:23. As Peter stated, *"And it shall come to pass in the last days, says God, that I will pour out of My Spirit on all flesh; your sons and your daughters shall prophesy, your young men shall see visions, your old men shall dream dreams. And on My menservants and on My maidservants I will pour out My Spirit in those days."* Acts 2:17–18.

The *"latter rain"* of Joel 2:23 is the outpouring of the Holy Spirit during the *"time of the end"* (Daniel 12:4), or *"last days"* (Acts 2:17). Without the latter rain, God's people—those who *"keep the commandments of God"* (Revelation 14:12)—will not grow to spiritual maturity, and will not be able to faithfully stand, and prevail, through the final time of trouble. The latter rain prepares God's people to remain faithful to Him during the persecution resulting from rejecting the Beast's mark, and to withstand the seven last plagues. It also gives them power to be witnesses for God, and to proclaim His message. Finally, it ripens the grain for a massive harvest at the closing work of the gospel. Remember, however, that unless the *"former rain"*, (Joel 2:23) occurs to water the *"baby seeds,"* as it did on the Day of Pentecost, the latter rain will yield no harvest.

Consider This ### Purified, Made White, and Refined

The followers of Christ will receive the outpouring of the Holy Spirit during the time of the end. The Scripture identifies this as the Latter Rain. During this Latter Rain, the Spirit of God will be poured out in great measure—just as it was at Pentecost when the Holy Spirit, symbolized by tongues of fire, fell on 120 disciples in the Upper Room. This is what Daniel refers to in verse 7, *"And when the power of the holy people has been completely shattered."*

The Hebrew word for *shattered* is "naphats," which can also mean "dispersed." The witness of God's people, in both word and action, will disperse the power of the Holy Spirit throughout the world. The witness to the world will be that God's people are willing to follow His Word and to keep His Sabbath, as He has commanded. Their characters will be tried by opposition from the wicked: *"Many shall be purified, made white, and refined."* Daniel 12:10. In preparation for the Second Coming of Christ, we must be cooperating with the Holy Spirit in developing our characters now.

The Bible states that *"the wicked shall do wickedly"* (Daniel 12:10), culminating in Revelation 13 and 14 with the Mark of the Beast. The Beast power (Papal Rome) will enforce a mark upon all people, and the price for choosing to reject the mark will be grave punishment. Initially, those who do not have this mark will not be able to buy or sell, but eventually they will be subjected to a death decree. Remember, however, that in the third of the five wonders, God's people will be delivered.

Daniel 12:11 — 1,290 Days

"And from the time that the daily sacrifice is taken away, and the abomination of desolation is set up, there shall be one thousand two hundred and ninety days."

Daily Sacrifice and Abomination of Desolation

Key to Prophecy There are more time prophecies in Daniel 12 than any other book of the Bible. The angel Gabriel continues doing what he has done in previous chapters, repeating and enlarging, so that Daniel would understand the work of the Papal power in the last days.

The day-for-a-year principle, i.e., the principle that a day in time prophecy represents one literal year, also applies when interpreting this prophecy (see Ezekiel 4:6; Numbers 14:34). The angel Gabriel began the prophecy in verse 12 with the rise of the Papacy, when Clovis I, king of the Franks, overthrew the Visigoths in 508 A.D. Clovis had converted to Catholicism, becoming the first Catholic king of France. He made Catholicism the National Church of France, and outlawed all others. He then made religious laws equal to civil laws of the state. Therefore, true worship of God was jointly changed through legislation by Clovis (State) and the Church (Catholicism). This gave birth to the Papacy as a civil power in 508 A.D., as had been foretold in Scripture. A mere 30 years later, in 538 A.D., the Church showed her authority by passing a Sunday Law, and enforcing her dogmas via civil power (see Daniel 11:31). Thus began the 1,260 years of Papal supremacy that Gabriel foretold in Daniel 12:7. This is the time Christ spoke of in Matthew 24:15, *"'Therefore when you see the "abomination of desolation," spoken of by Daniel the prophet, standing in the holy place' (whoever reads, let him understand)."*

In Daniel 8:13, 11:31, and 12:11, the word "daily" comes from the Hebrew word *tamid*, which means "regularly." Since the sacrifice was offered daily, or regularly, the word "sacrifice" was supplied for clarity.

In each situation, whether it be Pagan Rome, Papal Rome, or the revived Papal Roman Power of the last days, the daily sacrifice is taken away, and the abomination of desolation is set up. What has Roman Catholicism taken away that the Lord asks us to do on a regular basis? *"Remember the Sabbath day, to keep it holy. Six days you shall labor and do all your work, but the seventh day is the Sabbath of the Lord your God."* Exodus 20:8–11.

Not only has Catholicism done away with the Sabbath, but just as the

Bible prophesies, she set up the abomination of desolation—a day that was dedicated to a pagan god, and put in place of the Sabbath of the Lord.

In a statement placing the church above Scripture, she states: "The authority of the church could therefore not be bound to the authority of the Scriptures because the church had changed ... the Sabbath into Sunday, not by a command of Christ but by its own authority." (From Gaspare [Ricciulli] de Fosso, the Archbishop of Reggio's address in the 17th sessions of the Council of Trent, Jan. 18, 1562. Quoted by J. H. Holtzman, *Latin Canon and Traditions,* p. 263.)

The Papal power would arise in 508 A.D., last for 1,290 years, and come to its end in 1798 A.D. History records the event as follows: "General Berthier, [Napoleon's general], marched to Rome, entered it unopposed, on the 13th of February, 1798, and proclaiming a republic, demanded of the pope the renunciation of his temporal authority. Upon his refusal, he Pope Pius VI, was taken prisoner, and on the 20th of February, was escorted from the Vatican to Siena." (*Encyclopedia Britannica,* 11th edition, Vol. 21, p. 686). The end of the Papal rule, in 1798 A.D., marks the beginning of the period known in Bible prophecy as "the time of the end."

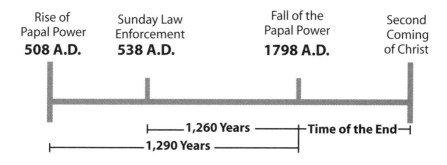

Daniel 12:12 — 1,335 Days

"Blessed is he who waits, and comes to the one thousand three hundred and thirty-five days."

The Blessing

Concerning the transgression of desolation, Daniel 8:13 asks how long the vision would last. The response was, *"two thousand three hundred days.*" From our study of Daniel 9, we found that the 2,300 days ended in 1844 A.D., at which time, according to Scripture, the Judgment began in Heaven. Just prior to that time, in 1843, a message would be proclaimed that would explain the abomination of desolation, and the blessing that comes to God's people who walk in the light of His word. This prophecy of Daniel 12:12 ties-in with the one in Daniel 9.

The fact that verse 12 begins by stating, *"Blessed is he who waits,"* shows that verses 11 and 12 are related, and that both time periods began simultaneously. The time periods began with the rise of the Papal Power in 508 A.D., and the 1290 years would extend until 1798, when the Papacy came to an end. The 1,335 years, starting at the same time as the 1290 years, would continue for another 45 years, bringing us to 1843 A.D. There was to be a special blessing to the followers of the Lord at that time.

Remember, Daniel's main concern was with God's people, and what would happen to them. History reveals that in 1843 A.D., a special message began to be preached—a message designed to prepare the world for the Second Coming of Christ. At that time, a group called the Millerite Movement began proclaiming three distinct messages that are recorded in Revelation 14, and which are known as the Three Angels' Messages. These messages are to be given during the time of the end, and to carry a special blessing to those who are preparing to meet the Lord.

The first angel proclaims that the hour of God's Judgment is come, and is now in session in Heaven (see Revelation 14:6–7). In Daniel 7:13, this is described as Christ coming before His Father as our Mediator during the Judgment. He stands in our place, so that we do not come into judgment, but pass from death unto life (John 5:24). What a marvelous blessing!

The second angel announces that Babylon, which symbolizes all false worship, is fallen, and invites God's people to "come out of her," in order to avoid her plagues, and to enjoy the blessing of following the Lord (see Revelation 14:8).

The third angel proclaims victory over the Beast, the Image, and the Mark (see Revelation 14:9–12). The blessing comes by being patient in keeping God's commandments, by living through faith in Jesus Christ, and by not receiving the Mark of the Beast, once it is legislated and enforced: *"And I saw something like a sea of glass mingled with fire, and those who have the victory over the beast, over his image and over his mark and over the number of his name, standing on the sea of glass, having harps of God."* Revelation 15:2.

Since 1843, these three angels' messages have been preached around the globe; and today, millions of people are receiving the blessing, and rejoicing in the hope of the soon return of Jesus. God's people have a solemn mission to proclaim these messages during the time of the end, shining as a light, reflecting the fruits of the Spirit, and causing others to desire to walk in the light in order to be ready to meet the Lord.

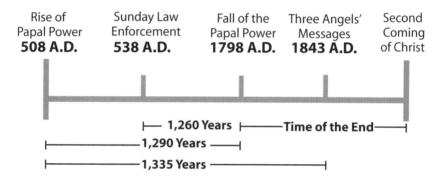

Daniel 12:13 — Till the End

"But you, go your way till the end; for you shall rest, and will arise to your inheritance at the end of the days."

 ### Stand in Your Lot

Daniel lived a wonderful, faithful life, during which he served as prime minister of two countries. Most importantly, however, he had a close relationship with his Lord, and was called "greatly beloved." Daniel 9:23; 10:11; 10:19.

For 70 years, Daniel had proclaimed the grace of God to the people of Babylon and Medo-Persia, but now the time had come for him to rest. One last time, the Lord reassured Daniel that he was loved, and that He had everything under control. The King James Version reads, *"And stand in thy lot at the end of the days,"* meaning that what Daniel was shown was predetermined to give guidance and encouragement to those living in the last days.

Daniel simply closed his eyes in the sleep of death, resting until the *"end of the days."* When he awakens at the end of time to see his Savior, and to receive his inheritance, it will seem to him but a mere moment has passed.

What a glorious day when all the righteous will be resurrected!

Prophecies Revealed To Daniel

605 B.C.	539 B.C.	331 B.C.	168 B.C.	538 A.D.	1798 A.D.	Second Coming of Christ
Daniel 2						
Head of Gold	Arms & Chest of Silver	Belly of Brass	Legs of Iron	Feet and Toes Iron and Clay Ten Divisions		"Days of these kings"
Babylon Dan. 2:38	Medo-Persia Dan. 2:39	Greece Dan. 2:39	Pagan Rome Dan. 2:40	Dan. 2:41-44		Dan. 2:44,45
Daniel 7					1844 A.D. The Court is Seated Dan. 7:9,10	
Lion	Bear	Leopard	Terrible Beast	Little Horn 1260 Years		Saints Possess the Kingdom Dan. 7:22
Babylon Dan. 7:4	Medo-Persia Dan. 7:5	Greece Dan. 7:6	Pagan Rome Dan. 7:7	Papal Rome Dan. 7:24,25		
Daniel 8						
	Ram Medo-Persia Dan. 8:20	Goat Greece Dan. 8:21	Little Horn — Both Pagan and Papal Rome Dan. 8:9-12			
Daniel 9	457 B.C. Decree to Restore and build Jerusalem		27 A.D. 31 A.D. 34 A.D. Baptism of Jesus — Gospel to the Gentiles — Crucifixion of Christ Dan. 9:27		1844 A.D. Judgment Began in the Heavenly Sanctuary	
	70 weeks or 490 years Dan. 9:24					
	69 weeks or 483 years Dan. 9:25		One Week 7 years			
	2300 years of Daniel 8:14 Began the Cleansing of the Sanctuary					
Daniel 11					Deadly Wound	Deadly Wound Healed King of the North Dan. 11:40-45
	Medo-Persia Dan. 11:1,2	Greece King of the North Dan. 11:3-13	Pagan Rome Dan. 11:14-29	Papal Rome Dan. 11:30-39		
Daniel 12				508 A.D. 538 A.D. Birth of Papacy	1798 A.D. 1943 A.D. Time of the End	
				1260 Years Dan. 12:7		
				1290 Dan. 12:11		
				1335 Dan. 12:12		

CALLED TO SERVE

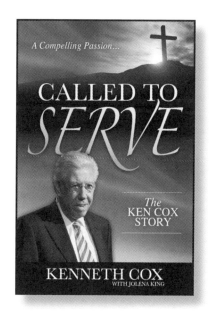

This book is about the amazing grace and mercy of God—and a man whose heart beats with compassion for sinners. As you read about the life of evangelist Kenneth Cox you'll be amazed how God took his life's darkest moments and turned them into his most precious assets.

A candid and fascinating autobiography, this is the story of a simple "Oakie" from Oklahoma who bravely faced a lifetime of trials and heartaches: a serious childhood illness, a mother debilitated by a brain tumor, an abusive father, and the loss of a spouse and an infant son. With rare grace (and humor) he's dealt with everyone from angry drug dealers to a cigarette-smoking deacon, winning them over with his compassion and unconditional love.

This is a glimpse into the life of a man who has led thousands to the foot of the cross in 17 different countries, risking his reputation and even his life to reach those whom Christ died for. It will keep you turning the pages—laughing and crying by turns—and ultimately inspire you to do more for the Master!

Price $16.99

REVELATION
PURE AND SIMPLE

This book on Revelation was not written for the theologian or Bible scholar. It was written for the man on the street—the man who's been told that Revelation is so full of symbolism that it cannot be understood. It was also written for those who have been told the events of Revelation have already passed and do not apply to us; that they will all take place in the future, long after we're gone; or that we will not be on earth when they take place—and a dozen other excuses for not understanding the truths that Jesus said we could and should.

It was written for the person who has a desire to know what Christ told John concerning the days we live in and for the person who wants to see the unfolding of prophecy, as one event after another takes place—each prophecy expanding and enlarging the next.

As you walk through Revelation, chapter by chapter in this easy reading format, your eyes will be opened to the roles played by different nations of the world.

Expect a blessing as you read, listen, and keep the things written in this book.

You can depend on it, for He promised it!